BASICS OF
CHRISTIANITY

THE BIBLE

Embracing God's Truth

MAX ANDERS

Publishers Since 1798

THOMAS NELSON PUBLISHERS
Nashville • Atlanta • London • Vancouver

Unless otherwise indicated, Scripture quotations are from the *New King James Version of the Bible*, © 1979, 1980, 1982, 1990, Thomas Nelson, Inc., Publishers.

Scripture quotations identified by NASB are from the *New American Standard Bible*, © 1960, 1962, 1963, 1968, 1971, 1973, 1975, by the Lockman Foundation, and used by permission.

Scripture quotations identified by NIV are from the *Holy Bible, New International Version*, © 1973, 1978, 1984 by International Bible Society, and used by permission of Zondervan Bible Publishers.

Scripture quotations identified by PHILLIPS are from *The New Testament in Modern Speech: Revised Edition*, © 1972 by Macmillan, and used by permission.

Library of Congress Cataloging-in-Publication Data

Anders, Max, 1943–
    The bible : embracing God's truth / Max Anders.
        p.   cm. — (We believe! series)
    Includes bibliographical references.
    ISBN 0–8407–1926–4
    1. Bible—Evidences, authority, etc.   2. Bible—Introductions.
3. Bible—Theology. 4. Bible—Hermeneutics. 5. Bible—Criticism,
interpretation, etc. I. Title. II. Series.
BS480.A63   1955
220.6′1—dc20   95-42821
                                                                                              CIP

Printed in the United States of America

1 2 3 4 5 6 7 8—00 99 98 97 96 95

Contents

Introduction to the
We Believe!
Basics of Christianity Series

In his book *Mere Christianity*, C. S. Lewis, a well-known Christian writer from Great Britain wrote:

> Everyone has warned me not to tell you what I am going to tell you . . . They all say "the ordinary reader does not want Theology; give him plain practical religion." I have rejected their advice. I do not think the ordinary reader is such a fool. Theology means "the science of God," and I think any man who wants to think about God at all would like to have the clearest and most accurate ideas about Him which are available. You are not children: why should you be treated like children?
>
> Theology is practical. Everyone reads, everyone hears things discussed. Consequently if you do not listen to Theology, that will not mean that you have no ideas about God. It will mean that you have a lot of wrong ones—bad, muddled, out-of-date ideas. For a great many of the ideas about God which are trotted out as novelties today, are simply the ones which real Theologians tried centuries ago and rejected. To believe in the popular religion of modern England (or America) is retrogression—like believing the earth is flat (135–136).

We want to be sure, as we navigate the sea of life, that we are not thinking we might drop off the edge, or that monsters lurk in the deep, or that the stars determine our destiny. We must think accurately. We must have truth. We must anchor ourselves to reality. Anything else is not only retrogression; it is unfulfilling, self-defeating, and even dangerous.

That is why this series was written. We are in a time of unprecedented upheaval in American culture. For over two centuries, many who lived in the United States believed in God and had a basic understanding of the Bible. But today, after one or two short generations of rapid social change, masses of Americans know nearly nothing about the Bible. When these people come into the church, they are not grounded in the same teachings as those who have grown up in the church. The result is a congregation of people who do not share a common knowledge base. And any group that lacks such a base cannot experience complete unity, and it cannot easily move in one direction as a congregation.

The lack of knowledge common to all members hampers a church's effectiveness in three other cases: First, new people come into the church thinking they know the truth about God, Jesus, and the Bible, but they don't. They picked up inaccurate information before coming into the church. Now they can be divisive, perhaps innocently, and can lead others into error.

Second is the case when Christians know quite a bit about one subject, but very little about another. For example, they may be interested in prophecy but know almost nothing about the deity of Christ. These are vulnerable to error about Jesus Himself, and despite their enthusiasm for prophecy (or it could be any other doctrine), their personal life is weakened, as well as the life of their church.

Third, churches today often are made up of people with several to many different church backgrounds. In the diversity of experiences lies precious strength, but only as that diversity arises from a common core of belief about Christian essentials. If any church is to be successful, the core of the congregation must together build upon a common base of accurate knowledge that corresponds to the One who is Truth. I hope that this series of books will help churches all across America (and even around the world) provide this crucial base of knowledge and thus be more securely attached to the church's Head, Jesus Christ.

One final word about how to use the book. It is structured so that an individual can go through it on his or her own or so that it can be used by a small group or Sunday school class. Please note the end-of-chapter reviews (Speed Bumps!), self-tests (Fill in the Blank), discussion questions, guided further study, and so on. Whether you are using the book alone or with a group, I hope that you will use this material to help you get the most out of the book.

The Fill in the Blank feature is, as you will see, a "no brainer." It doesn't take a rocket scientist to fill in the blanks. The purpose is not that you would memorize any answers but that the mental "speed bump" will slow you down enough so that you review what you should take away from the chapter. These features are simple, but effective, according to the many people who have used similar features in other books.

This series does not contain everything that a Christian ought to know, by any means. But a Christian should not know less. Therefore, it is to the good of the church, the body of Christ, that this series of books is dedicated. To God be the glory!

How To Teach This Book

The books in this series are written so that they can be used as a thirteen-week curriculum, ideal for Sunday school classes or other small-group meetings. You will notice that there only twelve chapters—to allow for a session when you may want to do something else. Every quarter seems to call for at least one different type of session, because of holidays, summer vacation, or other special events. If you use all twelve chapters, and still have a session left in the quarter, have a fellowship meeting with refreshments, and use the time to get to know others better. Or use the session to invite newcomers in hopes they will continue with the course.

All ten books in the series together form a "Basic Knowledge Curriculum" for Christians. Certainly Christians would eventually want to know more than is in these books, but they should not know less. Therefore, the series is excellent for seekers, for new Christians, and for Christians who may not have a solid foundation of biblical education. It is also a good series for those whose biblical education has been spotty.

Of course, the books can also be used in small groups and discipleship groups. If you are studying the book by yourself, you can simply read the chapters and go through the material at the end. If you are using the books to teach others, you might find the following guidelines helpful:

1. Begin the session with prayer.

2. Consider having a quiz at the beginning of each meeting over the self-test from the chapter to be studied for that day. The quiz can be optional, or the group may want everyone to commit to it, depending on the setting in which the material is taught. In a small disciple-

ship group or one-on-one, it might be required. In a larger Sunday school class, it might need to be optional.

3. At the beginning of the session, summarize the material. You may want to have class members be prepared to summarize the material. You might want to bring in information that was not covered in the book. There might be some in the class who have not read the material, and this will help catch them up with those who did. Even for those who did read it, a summary will refresh their minds and get everyone into a common mind-set. It may also generate questions and discussion.

4. Discuss the material at the end of the chapters as time permits. Use whatever you think best fits the group.

5. Have a special time for questions and answers, or encourage questions during the course of discussion. If you are asked a question you can't answer (it happens to all of us), just say you don't know, but that you will find out. Then, the following week, you can open the question and answer time, or perhaps the discussion time, with the answer to the question from last week.

6. Close with prayer.

You may have other things you would like to incorporate, and flexibility is the key to success. These suggestions are given only to guide, not to dictate. Prayerfully, choose a plan suited to your circumstances.

*Give me a Bible and a candle and shut me up
in a dungeon and I will tell you what the
world is doing.*
■ Cecil Dichard

How Important Is the Bible?

Just to the west of Jackson Hole, Wyoming, there lies a vast and imposing fortress of stone called the Grand Teton Mountains. Long and narrow, rising to nearly 14,000 feet, they stretch for fifty miles north and south like the sawtoothed backbone of a half-submerged prehistoric monster. One of the most pho-
tographed places in the United States, these mountains rise abruptly from a flat floor and cast their cold and impersonal, yet strikingly beautiful, presence in every direction for scores of miles.

> The Bible, like a massive mountain range, confronts the traveler of life and can't be wished away.

The Teton range is virtually impassable. If the summer is warm, there is one pass that will open for a matter of weeks to let you travel east and west over the backbone. Otherwise, you may have to drive as many as fifty or more miles out of your way to go west from Jackson Hole, just to get around one of the largest outcroppings of exposed stone in the world. When you look at the horizon anywhere near the area, the Tetons dominate the landscape.

In this chapter we learn that . . .

1. The Bible has played a major role in determining the social values of the Western world.
2. The Bible has been a dominant influence in the arts of the Western world.
3. The Bible has been a dominant influence in the spiritual, moral, and ethical formation of the Western world.

In the same way, when we scan the horizon of human civilization for the last two thousand years, we see the Bible, confronting the traveler like a massive mountain range that must be negotiated and can-

not be merely wished away. The Bible is an enormous historical presence, the dominant piece of literature and a dominant influence in history since the time of Christ. No other piece of literature has come within a fraction of its impact. If the Bible is a mighty oak, then every other piece of literature is a sapling, a seedling, or an acorn.

The curious, the earnest, the zealous traveler on life's highway wants to know about and seriously consider the claims of such a book. Why is the Bible so important?

What Influence Has the Bible Had on Our Society?

The Bible has played a major role in determining the social values of the Western world.

The Bible has made a monumental impact on our society, and we can be glad it has. Once a South Sea Islander proudly displayed his Bible to an American soldier during World War II. "We've outgrown that sort of thing," the soldier said. The Islander smiled back and said, "It is a good thing that we haven't. If it weren't for this book, we would have eaten you by now."

Whether the story is true or not, it certainly expresses a truth: If it weren't for the Bible, something, somewhere, may very well have eaten us by now, literally or otherwise.

The Bible is certainly the dominant piece of literature worldwide, with multiple billions of copies published to this point, and millions more published every year. While its impact may be diminishing in some circles, it is growing in others, and its historic impact cannot be denied. As one example, the United States was founded largely on Judeo-Christian principles drawn from the Bible, and when one considers the unprecedented historic impact which this nation has had on the world in the nineteenth and twentieth centuries in promoting peace and political freedom, it is clear that the influence of the Bible extends far beyond its borders.

The Bible has influenced many societies to adopt basic, important community virtues and to oppose several social vices.

The Family

In some parts of the world, a husband may have more than one wife. In some parts of the world, a man's wife is his property, to treat as he sees fit. In some parts of the world, if a couple produce a daughter when they wanted a son, they simply throw the daughter away. Not in America, however. Our laws governing the family have been forged on quite a different anvil.

The Bible has defined relationships in the family for the last two thousand years. Modern society has largely ignored biblical teachings about the family, and has, as a consequence, seen the family suffer. Yet numerous voices today are calling us back to the ideal, insisting that a society flourishes only to the extent that its families flourish.

> **The Bible's ideal of one man and one woman married for life provides the strongest underpinning for any society.**

The Bible's ideal of one man and one woman married to each other for life provides the strongest underpinning for any society. The Bible proclaims the dignity of man, woman, and child. Men and women are equals in the sight of God, and the value of women is upheld in the Christian Bible to a degree higher than that of any other religion's scriptures. The Bible is often misused, as well as falsely accused of being demeaning to women. Seen clearly, however, nothing could be farther from the truth.

Why I Need to Know This

If I do not understand how important the Bible is . . .

1. I may dismiss its importance in my life because I underestimate its importance throughout history.
2. I may miss the fact that any writing which has had the impact the Bible has had for the last two thousand years cannot be dismissed as "just another book." Its extraordinary influence on history requires explanation, and a curious person intent on knowing truth would want to understand what accounts for such influence.
3. I will miss the opportunity I have to learn and apply its wisdom in life. We are living in a time when the perceived value of the Bible for society, culture, and individuals is diminishing. I must understand the importance of the Bible so that I will know why I should champion the message of the Bible for society, culture, and the individual.

Jesus upheld the dignity and equality of women in His teaching and all His dealings with women. In Ephesians 5:25, the apostle Paul describes the love husbands are to give their wives by pointing to Christ, whose love for the church moved Him to give Himself up for her. Total and complete commitment to the welfare of the wife is the standard to which the Bible holds all husbands. The apostle Peter writes in 1 Peter 3:7, "husbands, dwell with [your wives] with understanding, giving honor." Whenever men have exploited women, they have violated the Bible, period.

So with children. Jesus held children in the highest esteem. Once "some children were brought to [Jesus] so that He might lay His hands on them and pray; and the disciples rebuked them. But Jesus said, 'Let the children alone, and do not hinder them from coming to Me; for the kingdom of heaven belongs to such as these'" (Matthew 19:13–14 NASB). The apostle Paul wrote "Fathers, do not provoke your children to wrath, but bring them up in the training and admonition of the Lord" (Ephesians 6:4). Also, in Colossians 3:21 we read, "Fathers, do not provoke your children, lest they become discouraged."

Certainly, it is true that the Bible has been used to justify the abuse of children with verses such as Proverbs 23:13–14: "Do not withhold correction from a child, / For if you beat him with a rod, he will not die. / You shall beat him with a rod, / And deliver his soul from hell." However, no one will abuse children on the basis of the Bible if he or she knows the whole Bible (not falling prey to the mistake of yanking verses like that out of context) and seeks to bring up children in the "nurture and admonition of the Lord." In fact, through the example and teaching of Jesus, children (just as women) are taken more seriously and treated more kindly in the Bible than they are in any other sacred writings. Protection of both the physical and psychological dimensions of women and children is a fundamental responsibility of all Christian men, and that is the origin of laws and customs governing life in America, in spite of all the violations we see. They are just that—violations, not the law.

Labor

Throughout history, the pendulum of conflict has swung back and forth between owners and workers. Whether it was masters and slaves, merchants and buyers, landowners and serfs, or employers and employees, there is a long history of persecution and victimization. The teaching of the Bible, in principle, ends the pendulum swings. First, it teaches us generally to "do unto others as we would have others do unto us." Second, it teaches us specifically concerning the responsibilities of employees and employers:

Slaves, be obedient to those who are your masters according to the flesh, with fear and trembling, in the sincerity of your heart, as to

Christ; not by way of eyeservice, as men-pleasers, but as slaves of Christ, doing the will of God from the heart. With good will render service, as to the Lord, and not to men, knowing that whatever good thing each one does, this he will receive back from the Lord, whether slave or free. And, masters, do the same things to them, and give up threatening, knowing that both their Master and yours is in heaven, and there is no partiality with Him (Ephesians 6:5–9 NASB).

Also, in Colossians we read,

Bondservants [applies also to employees] obey in all things your masters according to the flesh, not with eyeservice, as men-pleasers, but in sincerity of heart, fearing God. And whatever you do, do it heartily, as to the Lord and not to men, knowing that from the Lord you will receive the reward of the inheritance; for you serve the Lord Christ. Masters, give your bondservants what is just and fair, knowing that you also have a Master in heaven (3:22–24, 4:1).

If employees and employers followed these principles, the major pendulum swings between labor and management, to see who can take greatest advantage of whom, would disappear from the workplace.

Race Relations

In some countries, discrimination is accepted and deeply entrenched. Indeed, discrimination among races has been a particularly acute problem in America, though certainly not confined to America. Problems between African-Americans and Caucasians have certainly received the most attention, but conflict among Hispanics, Asians, Europeans, and Eastern Europeans has also been legendary in America. And, sad to say, it shows signs of getting worse in some places, instead of better. However, the laws of our country forbid racial discrimination because as a nation we believe that all people are created equal in the eyes of God. This value, while many people do not realize it, is part of our heritage from the Bible. Scripture lays discrimination to rest. Again, in general terms, Jesus' teaching of the Golden Rule applies: If we would not like to be discriminated against, then we should not discriminate. Specifically, in James

> **The Bible clearly establishes the equality of all people before God.**

2:8–9, we read, "If [in giving a seat of honor to a rich person] you are fulfilling the royal law, according to the Scripture, 'You shall love your neighbor as yourself,' you are doing well. But if you show partiality, you are committing sin and are convicted by the law as transgressors" (NASB).

These principles were violated in our nation in a ghastly display of selective understanding when we tolerated slavery. But, terrible as that was, at least it is no longer legal. And the breakdown of support for slavery was encouraged to a great extent by Christians. Today no one can claim support from the Bible to discriminate against another person. The Bible clearly establishes the equality of all people before God, and it is a sin to treat anyone otherwise.

Crime

What is considered to be lawful and unlawful in America has been influenced significantly by Scripture. Our law says we are not to steal, kill, cheat, or lie, just as the Ten Commandments also teach. According to the Bible, we are not even to covet, hate, or lust! People who don't know the Bible well have stereotyped ideas of what it teaches, thinking that it teaches intolerance, bigotry, and narrow-mindedness. The fact is, if everyone started following the Bible today, most of our major social problems would be solved, or well on their way, by tomorrow!

In addition, how we treat criminals is also influenced in a major way by the Scripture. Some countries punish thieves by chopping off a hand. Some routinely beat prisoners within an inch of their lives, merely on the whim of the authorities. Some countries exert no to little effort to give a suspect his due process under the law. In America, while some would say we have gone too far in the other direction, at least we treat everyone as innocent until proven guilty, and then still acknowledge that even criminals have some rights. These values have grown out of our national acceptance of a basically biblical view of human beings.

Humanitarianism

Poverty has always existed and always will exist. Even Jesus said, "the poor you have with you always" (Matthew 26:11 NASB). Yet the Bible has encouraged our national sense of compassion and directed us to help those who cannot help themselves. Christianity has done more for the poor, the needy, and the disadvantaged—and still does—than any other form of organized help in the world.

The Scriptures as the marching orders of believers have done more to advance humanitarianism than any other force on earth. From Mother Teresa helping the dying and destitute in the streets of Calcutta, to World Vision feeding thousands in a refugee camp, to the Salvation Army helping the down-and-outers, to the soup kitchens run by a rescue mission, to the church that provides shelter for the homeless, housing for unwed mothers, and financial assistance to those in crisis, Christianity is doing, and has done, more for the needy than any other institution or movement in the history of the world. The Bible, both Old and New Testaments, teaches that we should take care of those in our families, the poor, the needy, the hungry, and those who cannot help themselves.

> **The Bible teaches believers to care for their families, the needy, and those who cannot care for themselves.**

In the spirit of such teaching, from the earliest days of the church, through the Middle Ages, and into the modern age, Christianity has led the world in the establishing of hospitals, orphanages, and educational institutions. It has led the way in fighting slavery, child labor, and discrimination of any kind.

The oldest hospital in existence today is the Hotel Dieu (Hotel of God) in Paris, established by St. Landry around A.D. 600. Christians established the first hospital in the Western world in Rome, around A.D. 400. Today, throughout the world, hospitals named St. Joseph, St. Andrew, St. Anne, or the Baptist or Lutheran or Presbyterian or Methodist hospitals, testify the natural bent of Christian faith toward relieving human suffering and promoting health. The Bible gives the faith this direction.

Florence Nightingale established the institution of modern nursing out of her compassion and Christian convictions. The Red Cross and Young Men's Christian Association were established to extend Christian assistance to the needy. Louis Pasteur, a devoted follower of Christ, advanced medicine into the modern era as an outgrowth of his Christian convictions. Albert Schweitzer, as a result of his desire to serve Christ, spent his life helping establish a hospital in a remote part of Africa.

While excesses, miscalculations, and outright abuses have occurred throughout history in the name of Christ, those incidents are an embarrassment to Christ and a misapplication of biblical truth. In addition, the harm that has been done in the name of Christ comes nowhere near the good that has been done.

Government

There is no perfect government on earth, but the ideals of government in America as expressed in our Constitution and Bill of Rights surpass those of any government established before. By contrast, anti-Christian governments, from the Empire of Rome to Mussolini to Hitler to Stalin to Mao to a thousand obscure tyrants, have been murderous, barbarous expressions of the darkest corners of evil hearts. The Bible's influence on the establishment of benevolent governments has literally directed international fates. For example, if the United States had wanted to rule the world, it could have taken control at the close of World War II. After dropping the atomic bombs on Japan, the United States could have said to all other nations, "Unless you want one of these bombs dropped on the doorstep of your capitol, lay down your arms." But it didn't. Instead, it gave every country its freedom, and even spent billions rebuilding the very nations that waged war against us.

Christianity has had a profound effect on government in the world, especially in democracies. The dignity of the individual, the establishment of benevolent governments, and the promotion of just and fair laws is one of the great legacies of the Bible. It has promoted the humane treatment of criminals and has provided a safety net for disadvantaged people. Particularly in the history of England and the United States, the influence of Christianity has been profound. The major documents, from the *Magna Charta* to the *Mayflower Compact* to *The Declaration of Independence*, are filled with biblical principles and spirit. "We hold these truths to be self-evident: That all men are created equal; that they are endowed by their Creator with certain unalienable rights; that among these are life, liberty and the pursuit of happiness," is perhaps the most lofty ideal in all of the documents of all human governments.

The historic documents of Britain and the United States express biblical principles and spirit.

Education

Christianity has been the most powerful force for education in the history of the world. Christianity is a religion of the written word. The Bible is the record of the revelation which God wanted preserved for the good of humanity, and central to the ideal of Christianity is the spreading of education so that people can read and understand the Bible. Many of the languages of the world have been reduced to writing by missionaries so that the Bible could be translated into their language. Wycliffe Bible Translators, the world's largest Bible translation organization, has translated the Bible for millions upon millions of people since its inception. It has the goal of translating it for another three hundred million people who still do not have the Bible in their own language. The primary purpose of this mission is to spread the knowledge of Scripture, but it has the secondary result of promoting worldwide literacy.

The first printing press capable of mass production of literature, the Gutenburg Press, was invented to print the Bible, and the Bible was its first publication. It was the passion of the Reformers to put a Bible in the hands of as many people as possible. Many of Europe's finest schools were established to advance Christianity and a knowledge of Scripture.

In the United States, the same is even more evident. Nearly every early college was started for the expressed purpose of advancing the knowledge of Scripture and salvation. At the entrance to Harvard is a stone on which this inscription is found:

> After God had carried us safe to New England, and we had built our houses, provided necessities for our livelihood, reared convenient places for God's worship, and settled the civil government; one of the next things we longed for, and looked after was to advance learning, and perpetuate it to posterity; dreading to leave an illiterate ministry to the churches, when our present ministers shall lie in the dust.

Yale and Princeton were started for the same basic purpose. The Reverend John Witherspoon, the president of Princeton, once said, "Cursed be all learning that is contrary to the cross of Christ." Dartmouth was founded to train missionaries to reach the American Indians. The college of William and Mary was established that "the Christian faith might be propagated." In fact, every college or

Christianity has been the most powerful force for universal education in history.

university in the United States was founded for religious purposes until the University of Pennsylvania was established.

While colleges and universities have defected from their original purpose, nevertheless the Bible played a major role in the educating of Europe, England, and the United States. In addition, many Third World countries owe their educational heritage to religious education through schools established by missionaries.

If it were not for the Bible, the world would have many fewer literate peoples, and the level of literacy among the literate would be much lower. Certainly no other force or movement in history that we know has exerted such an influence.

In *The Bible and Civilization*, Gabriel Sivan wrote

More than any other code, past or present, the Bible has urged men and women imbued with a social conscience to tackle the age-old problems of poverty, suffering, and inequality. William Wilberforce fought slavery; Florence Nightingale reformed nursing and Elizabeth Fry prison conditions; Lord Shaftesbury protected the juvenile laborer; Lewis Gompertz pioneered animal welfare; William Booth's Salvation Army redeemed men from the gutter; Jean Henri Dunant made the Red Cross a delivering angel for the victims of war. Millions of underprivileged persons in country after country have been rescued from squalor and misery thanks to the humanitarian instincts and philanthropic work of great idealists [who got their inspiration from the Bible].

What Influence Has the Bible Had on Our Culture?

The Bible has been a dominant influence in the arts of the Western world.

Charles Colson, in his marvelous volume, *Loving God*, told the story of Telemachus, a fourth-century Christian. He was a peace-loving, beauty-loving man who lived in a remote village, tending his garden and spending much of his time in prayer. One day he thought he heard the voice of God telling him to go to Rome, so he obeyed, setting out on foot. Weeks later, he arrived wearily in the city at the time of a great festival. The little monk followed the crowd surging down the streets into the Coliseum. He saw the gladiators stand before the emperor and say, "We who are about to die salute you." Then he realized these men were going to fight to the death for the entertainment of the crowd. He cried out, "In the name of Christ, stop!"

As the games began, he pushed his way through the crowd, climbed over the wall, and dropped to the floor of the arena. When the crowd saw this tiny figure rushing to the gladiators and saying "In the name of Christ, stop!" they thought it was part of the show and began laughing.

When they realized it wasn't, the laughter turned to anger. As he was pleading with the gladiators to stop, one of them plunged a sword into his body. He fell to the sand. As he was dying, his last words were, "In the name of Christ, stop!"

Then a strange thing happened. The gladiators stood looking at the tiny figure lying there. A hush fell over the Coliseum. Way up in the upper rows, a man stood and made his way to the exit. Others began to follow. In silence, everyone left the Coliseum.

The year was A.D. 391, and that was the last battle to the death between gladiators in the Roman Coliseum. Never again in the great stadium did men kill each other for the entertainment of the crowd.

The Christian in tune with Scripture will love the beautiful and hate the hideous. God is a God of beauty, and hideousness belongs to the devil. Christians ought, then, to be lovers of beauty, and throughout history, Christians have led the world in the production of beauty through the arts.

Art

The Bible has given art its greatest themes. The creation, fall, and redemption of mankind; the great miracles of the Old Testament; the coming to earth of God as Jesus of Nazareth, born in a manger, heralded by angels, living a life of wisdom, power, compassion and sacrifice, and finally, being killed because of His goodness, and His return to earth at some time in the future; all present artists with the greatest possible themes.

> **The Christian in tune with Scripture will love the beautiful and hate the morally hideous.**

Christian art began to flourish under the protection of Roman Emperor Constantine in Byzantium (later called Constantinople and then modern Istanbul) after the first three hundred years following Christ's death. Byzantine art was very flat and representative. Then, during the Renaissance, the golden age of art was ushered in, and the biblical themes were painted as never before and never again. Michelangelo painted the incomparable Sistine Chapel and carved from stone Jesus dead in the arms of his grieving mother, Mary.

Raphael painted hundreds of Christian scenes, including some three hundred of the Virgin Mary. Leonardo da Vinci gave us the Last Supper, and Rembrandt filled our eyes with the interplay of dark and light, portraying perhaps the most touching scene of Jesus being taken down from the cross after His death.

All one has to do is leaf through a book on the history of art to see that Scripture has provided the greatest themes in all of history for art and has encouraged much of the finest art of the world.

In the twentieth century, the secularism that crept in and manifested itself from the acceptance of Darwinism to the near banishment of religious expression from all public arenas has manifested itself in a profound degeneration in art. Abandoning the images and themes of the Bible, much modern art consciously rejects Christian categories and reflects the breakdown of laws, meaning, and morals which typifies our modern society. You can watch America defect from the faith and begin to self-destruct just by leafing through a book on the history of art in America.

Scripture has inspired the greatest visual art and music of history.

Music

The same thing is true of all other art forms. Much great music of the past was distinctly Christian. The haunting Gregorian chant is the focal point of earliest preserved music. The Reformation brought newly evolving music into the church, with Luther's "A Mighty Fortress Is Our God" being the best known example. The next period, the Baroque period, saw music ascend to heights never before reached and, some would say, never again. Johann Sebastian Bach (1685–1750) and George Frideric Handel (1685–1759) were devout Christians whose music was composed for the glory of God. Handel's *Messiah* has ministered to millions, being performed each Christmas by thousands of orchestras and choirs across the world.

Bach is recognized by many as the greatest composer that ever lived. Much of his music was overtly Christian, with titles such as "St. Matthew's Passion," "St. John's Passion," "Jesus, Joy of Man's Desiring," and so on. And he often put initials on his music manuscripts such as *S.D.G.* which were initials for the Latin *Soli Deo Gloria*, meaning "glory to God alone." Other times he wrote *J.J.*, standing for *Jesu Juban*, meaning "Help me Jesus." He dedicated some of his works *I.N.J.* standing for *In Nomine Jesu*, meaning "In Jesus' Name."

Bach's influence is so pervasive that Beethoven, Haydn, Mendelssohn, Mozart, and many others reveal their debt to him in their own musical contributions. It is generally agreed that Bach is to music what Shakespeare is to literature—each the highest practitioner of his art form.

Some of the great music masters following Bach were Christians, but most were not, and we see, as in art and literature, a steady decline in music from that time on, reaching the low point in our modern era. Many music lovers and experts would disagree, but I agree with Francis Schaeffer, who showed that decline in music, art, and literature parallels the decline in overall devotion to God. Bach and others like him, however, laid the foundation for modern Western music, and this foundation came out of the church and from the Scriptures, for the most part.

Literature

The Bible's influence on the literature of the Western world since the Middle Ages is simply immeasurable. Not only has literature drawn upon the Bible as a source for themes and stories, but it has also been heavily influenced by the Bible's images, phrases, and characters when these were not even its main subject matter. In fact, the Bible's influence on literature is so great that, in the words of the literary scholar Northrop Frye, "a student of English literature who does not know the Bible does not understand a great deal of what is going on in what he reads." Today courses in the Bible are offered in many university English departments in order to equip students adequately for their study of literature, since many students now arrive at college with little knowledge of the Bible.

Read any great work of Western literature from the Middle Ages to this century, and you will invariably discover that the Bible provides either its subject matter or a variety of influences. Consider a handful of noteworthy examples: Augustine's

Confessions, the first modern autobiography, tells of the role of the Bible in his own conversion to Christ. The mystery and morality plays of the medieval church, of which *Everyman* is the outstanding example, enact scenes and themes from the Bible for the edification of worshipers. Both Dante's *The Divine Comedy* and Chaucer's *The Canterbury Tales* exhibit enormous influence from the Bible, as do the works of Shakespeare, John Milton, Edmund Spenser, and many other poets, dramatists, and novelists.

Examples from the last two centuries include the works of Charles Dickens, Nathaniel Hawthorne, James Joyce, Robert Louis Stevenson, Leo Tolstoy, Mark Twain, Fyodor Dostoevsky, William Faulkner, T. S. Eliot, Thomas Mann, C. S. Lewis, J.R.R. Tolkien, Willa Cather, and Flannery O'Connor—and the list could be expanded to include every significant author of Western literature. As scholar Leland Ryken points out, beyond providing major substance to many poems, dramas, or works of prose fiction, the Bible continues to provide titles for works, such as *Go Down Moses* (Faulkner), *East of Eden* (John Steinbeck), *The Sun Also Rises* (Ernest Hemingway), and *Go Tell It on the Mountain* (James Baldwin). Many authors draw from the Bible in creating and naming their characters. For example, John Milton transforms the biblical judge in the drama *Samson Agonistes*, and Hawthorne derives "Hester" in *The Scarlet Letter* from the biblical "Esther" and the name of her illegitimate child "Pearl" from the "pearl of great price" in Jesus' parable ("The Literary Influence of the Bible" 474). Through such echoes of the Bible, readers are urged to explore both the biblical sources and their relation to the poems, dramas, and stories that use them.

As we have seen for other areas of Western art and culture, the Bible's influence on literature is, in a word, ubiquitous—found everywhere at the same time. People who want to understand great works of Western literature must not only hold in one hand the literature they are reading, but also keep in the other the Bible of literature, which is nothing other than the Bible of Jewish and Christian faith. Without the Bible, people not only miss or misconstrue key elements of literary art, but worse, if they are themselves products of Western culture, they do not deeply understand either their own world or themselves.

What Influence Has the Bible Had on Our Spiritual Life?

The Bible has been a dominant influence in the spiritual, moral, and ethical formation of the Western world.

The child's game, pin the tail on the donkey, is predicated upon one simple reality. When you can't see, unpredictable things happen. In a child's game, those unpredictable things are harmless and humorous. In case you are not familiar with the game, there is a picture of a donkey on a bulletin board. This poor donkey, however, is missing its tail. One child is blindfolded, given a tail with a pin sticking through it (I think there are Velcro® versions now), twirled around several times so that he doesn't know which direction he's facing, and told to pin the tail on the donkey. The fun comes when all the children who can see get to watch the misguided attempts of the blindfolded child to get the tail in the right place. Not only does the child usually not get the tail in the right place, he often doesn't even get it on the donkey. It may end up on the donkey's nose, ear, belly, or even on a sofa, chair back, or between the shoulder blades of an unsuspecting playmate. Much is lost when you can't see.

This game is a metaphor for life. Truth is like light. Ignorance and falsehood are like darkness. With light, living life successfully is difficult. Without light, it is impossible! The fate of civilizations hangs on whether or not they will see the light beaming from the Bible and walk in its illuminated pathway.

Objective Truth

The Bible is important because it gives us objective truth. We are living in a day when there are those who say there is no such truth. In fact, Allan Bloom wrote in his profound book, *The Closing of the American Mind*, that the most common value held by nearly everyone today is that all truth is relative. In fact, if there is one thing we can be certain of, they say, it is that there is nothing they can be certain of.

The Bible expresses objective truth.

But do you know what happens if all truth is relative? What happens is that the blindfold goes on. Suddenly humanity cannot see. It is just as likely to pin the donkey's tail on the sofa as it is on the donkey. It is a dangerous world when you cannot see.

The person without truth has no answers for the great questions of life: Who am I?; where did I come from?; why am I here?; and where am I going? He has no basis for declaring something right or wrong, good or bad, beautiful or ugly, just or unjust. However, the instant the light is turned on, the danger is over. We see the donkey clearly, and the tail can be put in the right place.

Moral Standards

"Calvin and Hobbes" is a popular newspaper cartoon strip. Calvin is a little boy and Hobbes is his small stuffed tiger who becomes a large, real tiger whenever no one besides Calvin is around. One day as they were taking a walk through the woods, Calvin announced to Hobbes that he didn't believe in ethics anymore. As far as he was concerned, the ends justify the means. "Get what you can while the getting's good—that's what I say! Might makes right! The winners write the history books. It's a dog-eat-dog world, so I'll do whatever I have to and let others argue about whether it's 'right' or not."

At that moment, Hobbes pushes Calvin into a deep mud hole. Calvin yells, "Hey! Why'd you do that?"

Hobbes replies innocently, "You were in my way. Now you're not. The ends justify the means."

"I didn't mean for everyone, you dolt! Just me!" screams Calvin as he rises from the wallow, wiping mud off his face.

"Ahh. . . ," replies Hobbes as he strolls thoughtfully away.

Much of Calvin's blood flows through the veins of all of us. We want the freedom to do what we want, but don't want others to have that same freedom if it impacts us negatively. That is why we need the Bible. The Bible gives us moral standards which are necessary if we are to get along with each other. If it were not for God and the Bible, it is hard to tell how far civilization might degenerate. If everyone looks out only for himself, the law of the jungle becomes the law of the land . . . the survival of the fittest. Only as people willingly look out for one another can civilization advance. When Jesus said, "Do unto others as you would have others do unto you" (Luke 6:31), He voiced one of the most profound single sentences in the history of humanity. With acceptance of that one principle, many of humanity's greatest problems would disappear.

"If there is no God," wrote Dostoevsky in his great novel *The Brothers Karamazov*, "then all things are permissible." Francis Schaeffer, an evangelical theologian, spoke prophetically when he used to teach that unless you can appeal to God, there is no such thing as right and wrong. You say something is right, I say it is wrong. We cancel each other out. Only if there is a God, and if God has revealed right and wrong to us can we say something is right or wrong, good or bad, just or unjust.

> **"If there is no God, then all things are permissible."**

Hitler killed six million Jews and many Christians who tried to help them. Stalin killed over fifty million of his countrymen. Mao was responsible for perhaps as many as seventy million Chinese deaths. All three of these men were committed and reasoned atheists. Without God, the "rights and wrongs" of what we call civilized countries disappear. If there is no God, then there is nothing inconsistent with what these men did. You may not like it. You may prefer that they not have done it, but you cannot call it wrong. They thought it was right. So who are you to call them wrong? But if God calls them wrong, then you have something. There is leverage there.

Why do we need the Bible? Because right and wrong, good and bad, just and unjust disappear into a fog of formless gray without the Bible. Unless God has revealed to us a moral code, we have none except that which is imposed on us by whoever has enough power. Our light becomes darkness.

Life after Death

As we look at the great conveyor belt of life, we see people sitting on it out in front of us, and as they get to the end, they drop off. But we don't know where they go. Left to our own perceptions or knowledge, we have no confidence in knowing what happens when we die.

The Bible speaks convincingly of life after death, and tells us what we must do to prepare ourselves for eternal life. You don't hear much about it these days when tolerance is the number-one virtue, and objective truth is sacrificed on the altar of tolerance, but the Bible teaches that there is a heaven and a hell. Heaven is a place of eternal joy, and hell is a place of torment and eternal destruction.

If the Bible is wrong, then there is nothing to worry about. But if the Bible is right, there is plenty to worry about. If you don't like to go to the dentist, you will want nothing whatsoever to do with hell.

The Bible teaches that the only thing that separates us from God is sin. All have sinned and come short of the glory of God (Romans 3:23), and the wages sin earns is death, eternal separation from God (Romans 6:23). It teaches that there is forgiveness with God (Psalm 130:4) and that the one who comes to Jesus will not be turned away (John 6:37). The Bible also teaches that those who have Jesus, God's Son, have eternal life (1 John 5:12). Putting all that together, we conclude that we must come to Jesus, repent of our sins, ask Him to forgive our sins and give us eternal life, and come into our lives and make us the kind of people He wants us to be. That, and that alone, gets us to heaven. How good we are has nothing whatsoever to do with whether or not we get to heaven, because no one can be good enough. We must get there because we turn to Jesus, who will forgive us and give us eternal life if we will give our lives to Him.

The Bible speaks convincingly of life after death.

Changed Lives

An endless number of people testify to this remarkable fact: Their lives changed when they committed themselves to following the truth of the Bible. Jesus' disciples changed. Many well-known figures down through history changed. Millions of people today would say that their lives changed. And my life changed.

My greatest concern about becoming a Christian was that I had turned over new leaves before, but they never stayed "turned over." They always ended up flipping back to their original position. I was afraid of embarrassing myself and of doing God no favors by letting the cat out of the bag and announcing that I was a Christian. Then, losing the meaning of the moment of decision, I feared that I would slide back into the life I was living before.

But when I finally did take the plunge to become a Christian, I found a new power, a new presence, a new "something" in my life which the Bible tells me is the Holy Spirit. He would not let me go back to my old life. Sure, I have had relapses, as have nearly all Christians. But something alive within me is always there, pulling me back, convicting me of sin, calling me to righteousness, convincing me of truth, of the validity of righteousness, and the self-destructiveness of sin, making me want to please God and be like Him. My life has been changed by something, and when I read in the Bible that that is the ministry of the Holy Spirit, I realize that my experience conforms to the teaching and testimony of Scripture. Changed lives are the most powerful testimony to the importance of the Bible.

Conclusion

Why is the Bible so important? The Bible is, as I said earlier, a massive historical presence. Its influence on nearly every area of life is difficult to exaggerate. Suffice it to say, the world would be a darker, uglier, crueler place than we can imagine if it were not for the light, beauty, and love revealed in the Bible.

Speed Bump!
Slow down to be sure you've gotten the main points of this chapter.

*Q*uestion *A*nswer

Q1. What influence has the Bible had on our society?

A1. The Bible has played a major role in determining the social *values* of the Western world.

Q2. What influence has the Bible had on our culture?

A2. The Bible has been a dominant influence in the *arts* of the Western world.

Q3. What influence has the Bible had on our spiritual life?

A3. The Bible has been a dominant influence in the spiritual, moral, and ethical *formation* of the Western world.

Fill in the Blank

*Q*uestion *A*nswer

Q1. What influence has the Bible had on our society?

A1. The Bible has played a major role in determining the social _____ of the Western world.

Q2. What influence has the Bible had on our culture?

A2. The Bible has been a dominant influence in the _____ of the Western world.

Q3. What influence has the Bible had on our spiritual life?

A3. The Bible has been a dominant influence in the spiritual, moral, and ethical *formation* of the Western world.

For Discussion and Thought

1. If the Bible is a 10 on the scale of historical impact (10 being the highest) and the most significant book every written, what book do you think is number two?

2. If the Bible is a 10 on the scale of historical impact (0 meaning no historical impact, 10 meaning the impact level of the Bible), what number would you assign to your number two choice? What would you say about the difference?

3. How many people in our country do you think understand the impact the Bible has had on the way they think, their values, and their outlook on life?

4. Do you think that, if people understood the influence the Bible has had on Western thought and values, it would affect the way they value the Bible?

What If I Don't Believe?

1. If I don't believe the Bible's impact on the Western world, I am either undereducated or in denial of reality.

2. Many people, even Christians, don't realize how much the Bible has influenced our world because we take so many things for granted, and because our increasingly secularized education system is not interested in the religious basis of truth or is even hostile toward it. If I don't believe the importance of the Bible, I am like a pawn, being manipulated by a hostile or indifferent society into accepting an inaccurate picture of reality.

3. I risk the danger of underestimating the importance of the information the Bible presents, especially on how to live a meaningful life, how to be related to God, and how to prepare for life after death.

For Further Study

1. Scriptures

- Exodus 20:1–17
- Matthew 25:34–40
- Matthew 26:11
- Luke 6:31
- Romans 1:18–20
- 1 Corinthians 15:19
- 2 Corinthians 5:17
- James 2:8–9

Read these passages and consider how they add to your understanding of the information in this chapter.

2. Books

Several other books are very helpful for studying this subject further. They are listed below in general order of difficulty. If I could read only one of these, I would read the first one.

> *What If Jesus Had Never Been Born?* James Kennedy
> *The Church at the End of the Twentieth Century,* Francis Shaeffer
> *How Should We Then Live?* Francis Schaeffer
> *Surprised by Joy,* C. S. Lewis

2

If the Bible is not true religion, one is very
excusable in being deceived, for everything in
it is grand and worthy of God. The more I
consider the Gospel, the more I am assured
there is nothing there which is not beyond the
march of events and above the human mind.
■ **Napoleon Bonaparte**

Is the Bible the Word of God?

We are living in an incongruous time in American history. On one hand we do not believe that objective truth exists, but on the other, we are hungering for truth as never before. While we reject the concept of objective truth, we nevertheless believe that some things can be true for us. So Americans wolfishly search for truth that will guide them, whether or not it will guide anyone else. As a result, we explore a web of avenues in order to find truth that will work for "me."

Every year, the hottest-selling tabloid newspapers that infest the

Many Americans reject the idea of objective truth, yet they cling to the belief that some things can still be true for them.

checkout lanes of grocery stores are the year-end editions which contain all the prophecies by self-proclaimed psychics for the upcoming year. The prophecies range from the goofy to the bizarre to the absurd. Pope John Paul II was to have recorded a hit record with ex-Beatle, Paul McCartney; Hillary Clinton, President Clinton's wife, was to have had a baby, and so on. James Kennedy, pastor of Coral Ridge Presbyterian Church in Ft. Lauderdale, Florida, on his Sunday morning broadcast once said that he had saved these prophecies for one year, and then looked back to see how many of them came true. None of them did. Not one! Nevertheless, "inquiring minds" scoop them up like gold nuggets, and pore over them as though they were gospel.

Some try crystals; others, reincarnation; still others, channeling (getting in touch with spirits of people who have died) to try to find truth to live by. Probably the most popular means is astrology. The horoscope appears in nearly every major newspaper in the country. You can buy your horoscope at almost any grocery store checkout

stand. If you are wealthy enough, you can call psychic hotlines and as-
trologers advertised on television who promise you all you need to
know for success in business and love. Why people believe in predic-
tions which either do not come true or are too generalized to verify
whether or not they come true is beyond me. What influence the stars
could possibly have over our lives is inexplicable. Yet people flock to
astrology like seagulls to a shrimp boat.

This spiritual revival sweeping the United States is not, in large
measure, a revival of established religion. Rather, it is a renewal of
spiritual interest targeted toward unconventional and unorthodox beliefs.

In this chapter we learn that . . .

1. The Bible as originally written was without error.
2. The Bible that we have today says essentially the same thing that the
    original Bible said.
3. Not one archaeological find disproves accounts in the Bible and many
    confirm the historical accuracy of the Bible.
4. The fulfilled prophecies of the Bible lend powerful support to its being the
    word of God.
5. The hearts of multiplied millions of people throughout the last two
    thousand years have been transformed by the Bible, lending weight to its
    being the word of God.

In the face of all this, the Bible has been under severe attack, and
the confidence of many Christians and sympathizers of Christianity
has been needlessly shaken. Needlessly, because while no book ever
written has been attacked as viciously, for as long, and by as many
brilliant minds as the Bible has, it has proven to be indestructible. It is
an anvil that has destroyed many a hammer. It has been burned,
banned, and besmirched, yet it stands today stronger than ever.
Scrutiny of the Scriptures has only demonstrated its accuracy. Attempts to keep it from people have only made them more hungry for
it. New archaeological discoveries repeatedly confirm the historical reliability of the Bible. And the message of the Bible is being received,
worldwide, by nearly 90,000 people a day. The collapse of the Soviet
Union, where atheism was the official doctrine, has resulted in the
greatest turning to Christ in the history of the church. And in China,
where atheism is official and Christianity is still repressed in many
ways, there are an estimated thirty to eighty million Christians as of
this writing. If the repression of Christianity is ever lifted and we are

able to discover what is really going on in China, many mission experts believe that China will surpass, or perhaps already has surpassed Russia as the greatest turning to God in the history of the church. In parts of Asia, Latin America, and Africa, people are converting to Christianity at a rate exceeding the birth rate.

The Bible is a truth anvil that has shattered many a critic's hammer.

The greatest non-event of the twentieth century was the death of Christianity. It didn't happen. The theory of evolution, the establishment of Marxism, and the rise of scientific knowledge were supposed to drive the final nails in the coffin of Christianity. Just the opposite is true. Evolution is a theory in chaos, Marxism has collapsed under its own weight, and science is only confirming Christian truths rather than disproving them. All the while, Christianity is more a world force today than it ever was. It is not always easy for Americans to realize this because of the beating Christianity has taken here in the public arena in the twentieth century. But get a global perspective, and you'll see that atheism is on the way out! The Bible has outlived every critic and stands today stronger than ever. Billions of Bibles have been distributed, and millions more are being distributed every year.

What could possibly account for this astonishing hunger for, longevity of, and indestructibility of the Bible? The answer is that the Bible claims to be the word of God, and there is every reason to believe that claim. We want to look at some of those reasons in this chapter.

Does the Bible Contain Errors?

The Bible as originally written was without error.

If there were mistakes in the Bible, and the Bible were the word of God, then God would be the author of mistakes. If God is the author of mistakes, then He is not what the Bible claims He is. So if we are to rely on God, we must have a reliable Bible. We must have confidence that the Bible is a book without error.

Stated as plainly as possible, nothing in the Bible can be demonstrated to be an error of fact. People often are told, or get the impression, that errors or contradictions riddle the Bible, but everything that seems to be an error or contradiction can be explained. For example, Matthew only mentions one angel at the tomb after Jesus' resurrection (Matthew 28:1–8). Luke mentions two angels (Luke 24:4). This is not a contradiction, as some people claim. Wherever you have two angels, it is a mathematical necessity that you must also have one angel. If Matthew had said there was one and only one angel, then there would have been a contradiction, but he did not. He merely mentioned the angel who said the words that Matthew recorded.

In a more complex example, the four Gospels differ in their account as to what was written on a sign that was nailed to the cross above Jesus' head when He was crucified. Matthew says, "This is Jesus, the king of the Jews." Mark says, "The king of the Jews." Luke says, "This is the king of the Jews," and John says, "Jesus of Nazareth the king of the Jews." True, all of these are different. However, none of these accounts say that this was all that was written on the sign. The whole thing can be reconciled by realizing that the sign contained everything that was written: "This is Jesus of Nazareth, the king of the Jews." From this full statement, each author, for reasons of his own, articulated only part of the statement, but there is no error.

I may tell my wife that I am going to the post office. When I get home, I tell her that I picked up a screwdriver at the hardware store. Did I lie to her by not telling her I was going to the hardware store? No. I did go to the post office, and I did not tell her that I was going *only* to the post office. I did not give her all the truth, but everything I gave her was true.

The Bible expresses truth without error in the ways truth was expressed in ancient times.

Many people who say the Bible is a book of mythology, or that it is filled with contradictions and riddled with errors haven't read the Bible much or studied the issues at hand. They have not analyzed the Bible sufficiently in its own ancient context to examine its credibility. People base their whole eternity on an off-the-cuff comment by some professor in college or an unsubstantiated allegation by some colleague at work. How unwise! When we respond to such allegations or to any Bible difficulties we may discover, it is very important to remember two truths about the Bible: (1) God is true and faithful and never deceives or leads anyone astray, so we can trust that His word given to us in the Bible has the same qualities. (2) God's word was given through human authors who expressed it in the ways and manners that people of their times expressed truth, so we modern readers must learn those ways and keep them in mind as we read the Bible. The Bible is without error. Any apparent error or contradiction can be explained credibly.

Are the Bible Manuscripts Reliable?

The Bible that we have today says essentially the same thing that the original Bible said.

Ancient copies of the Bible or portions of the Bible that were hand-copied before the invention of the printing press are called manuscripts. Although some discrepancies in the various ancient manuscripts exist, they are insignificant, and have no bearing on any doctrine. For example, some of the discrepancies are like the difference between spelling the word color as "c-o-l-o-r" the way we do now, or "c-o-l-o-u-r," the British way of spelling it. Those kinds of discrepancies exist. There are also some discrepancies in numbers and words and occasional phrases. These variances are very few and affect no doctrine. According to Bruce Metzger, a New Testament scholar who taught at Princeton, after 2,000 years of being copied, only forty of the 20,000 lines in the New Testament are debatable today. Everything else is a given, and none of the variances affect the Christian faith.

Two other matters are important in establishing the reliability of the ancient manuscripts from which we get our English Bible: their number and their age. First, there are a ton of them. Of important ancient secular documents, only seven copies of Plato's *Tetralogies*, ten copies of Caesar's *Gallic Wars*, and 643 copies of Homer's *Iliad* exist. But there are over 5,000 ancient manuscripts of the New Testament! That is remarkable, indeed. In addition to the New Testament documents, we have over 10,000 ancient manuscripts or parts of manuscripts of the Old Testament. Of course, this multitude of manuscripts makes it easier to verify how accurately they have been copied and confirm what the original documents said. The Bible is easily the most common ancient document in existence, and by comparing this galaxy of manuscripts, we see that except for insignificant exceptions, they all say exactly the same thing. Our Bible today is reliable.

A second matter affecting the value of the manuscripts is their age. That is, how soon after the original was written were the copies made? In this regard, the New Testament manuscripts are again superior to other writings. For example, Caesar's *Gallic Wars* was written about 60 B.C., yet the earliest existing manuscript we have is dated A.D. 900, nearly 1,000 years later. Plato's *Tetralogies* was written in about 400 B.C., but the earliest manuscript dates to about A.D. 900, nearly 1,300 years later. And Homer's *Iliad* was written about 900 B.C., but the earliest copy we have dates to about 400 B.C., about 500 years later. The New Testament was completed no later than A.D. 100, yet the earliest known manuscript that contains most of the New Testament dates to about A.D. 200, a span of approximately 100 years. And some fragments date back as early as A.D. 125. Recently a manuscript fragment of the New Testament was dated to before A.D. 100, during the lifetime of the apostle John, who was himself an author of parts of the New Testament.

> **Evidence that the Bible has been preserved nearly perfectly for 2,000 years is greater than that available for any other book from ancient times.**

One final piece of information enhances the credibility of the Bible manuscripts. Many people have heard of the Dead Sea Scrolls, but do not know why they are so important. These scrolls were found in 1947 in a series of caves in a desolate area just west of the Dead Sea. Between 145 B.C. and A.D. 68, they were inhabited by a Jewish community protesting the leaders and practices they believed corrupted worship at the Jerusalem temple. For some reason, they stored a number of these scrolls in sealed jars, where they survived the ravages of time, so that many of them are readable today.

Why I Need to Know This

The Bible claims to be the word of God. I need to know if it makes sense to believe that it is. Blind faith is not a sufficient platform on which to place one's eternal destiny. If I can reasonably justify accepting the Bible as the word of God, then I have a compass for life, giving me instruction in how to live on earth and assurance of life after death in heaven with God.

When found, the Dead Sea Scrolls were one thousand years older than the previous earliest Old Testament manuscript. By comparing the manuscripts, we know that in one thousand years of copying, only one word in Isaiah 53, the word "light" in verse 11, differs from the earliest manuscript known previously, and this variation does not affect the meaning at all. So for all practical purposes, we know that the Old Testament manuscript remained unchanged from one thousand years earlier. This gives us great confidence in the reliability of Bible manuscripts.

In many cases, dedicated, scholarly monks copied these manuscripts. They viewed their task as a sacred labor of love. Some believed that a curse fell on anyone who added to or subtracted from the Scripture (Revelation 22:18–19). Therefore, they took exacting and painstaking measures to ensure accuracy in the process. This explains why variations in manuscripts hardly exist, and this is why we believe that the Bible we have today is, for all practical purposes, exactly the same as originally written.

How Does Archaeology Testify to the Accuracy of the Bible?

Not one archaeological find disproves accounts in the Bible and many confirm the historical accuracy of the Bible.

Many of the attacks on the accuracy of the Bible were begun prior to modern archaeology. However, beginning with major excavations in the Holy Land in the mid-1800s, archaeological evidence has confirmed the Bible's historical accuracy time and time again. As travel became easier and scholars more curious, archaeologists began to peel away the earth's surface to reveal ancient cities, painted tombs, solid gold likenesses of rulers, jars, money and items needed for the afterlife, tablets of stone and clay telling the story of a people or a city, and so on. As these artifacts piled up, references to biblical places and people surfaced. In a number of cases, people or places which skeptics had written off as fanciful mistakes in the Bible were confirmed. In fact, many things that eighteenth- and nineteenth-century scholars questioned have now been verified as factual, such as cities and things in those cities, rulers, and important people.

For example, Belshazzar, named in the book of Daniel as the last king of Babylon, was nowhere to be found in Babylonian records: all known Babylonian records listed Nabonidus as the last king. Then, archaeological records revealed that Nabonidus left Babylon for ten years and went to Arabia. In his absence, his son Belshazzar ruled as king in his place during the time of Daniel. In this way, archaeology explained the apparent discrepancy between the biblical record and the previous Babylonian record (Paul Little, *Know Why You Believe* 95).

> "No archaeological discovery has ever controverted a biblical reference."

Clifford Wilson, a committed Christian and retired archaeologist at the University of Sydney in Australia, tells of evidence of a man named Sanballat, found during the time of Alexander the Great. A man named Sanballat is also found in the book of Nehemiah, before Alexander the Great's time. Critics often cited this as proof of historical error in the Bible. But then it was discovered that there were three Sanballats, and that one of them lived during the time of Nehemiah. The Bible was right after all ("The Bible: Fable, Fraud or Fact," *Coral Ridge Video Ministry,* January 4, 1994).

More than a century of biblical excavations at over 25,000 sites have repeatedly confirmed the accuracy of the Bible. After working in the field for many years, noted archaeologist Nelson Glueck said, "It may be stated categorically that no archaeological discovery has ever controverted (contradicted) a biblical reference" (quoted in Josh McDowell, *Evidence that Demands a Verdict* 1:65).

To be completely candid, we must assess what all this means. By itself, this does not mean that the Bible is the word of God. It does mean that the Bible has never been proven wrong on any point of history or geography. However, the historical-geographical test must be passed if we are to conclude that the Bible is the word of God. Mistakes in the record would cause us to doubt the Bible as the word of God. Since there are no mistakes in it, it passes the historical-geographical test and allows us, on that ground, to conclude that it could be the word of God. Whether or not we decide it is the word of God is ultimately a matter of faith, but we would not be able to make that conclusion if we found the Bible riddled with error.

Does Fulfilled Prophecy Testify to the Identity of the Bible as the Word of God?

The fulfilled prophecies of the Bible lend powerful support to its being the word of God.

The Bible is the only book in the world that has specific prophecies clearly fulfilled hundreds of years after they were given. I addressed this issue in another volume in this series, *Jesus: Knowing Our Savior.* The prophecies that validated the deity of Jesus are exactly the same as those that validate the Bible as the word of God.

Jesus fulfilled many Old Testament prophecies, some of them more obvious than others. For our purposes, we will focus on the more obvious ones. So that you can see them most clearly, I state the Old Testament prophecy briefly, and then its fulfillment in the New Testament. Let the record speak for itself.

1. *Prophecy: The Messiah would be born of a virgin.* "Therefore the Lord Himself will give you a sign: Behold a virgin will be with child and bear a son, and she will call His name Immanuel" (Isaiah 7:14 NASB).

Fulfillment: Jesus was born of the virgin Mary. "She was found to be with child by the Holy Spirit. And Joseph . . . kept her a virgin until she gave birth to a Son; and he called His name Jesus" (Matthew 1:18–25 NASB).

2. *Prophecy: The Messiah would be born into the family of King David.* "Behold the days are coming, declares the LORD, when I shall raise up for David a righteous Branch; and He will reign as king and act wisely and do justice and righteousness in the land" (Jeremiah 23:5 NASB).

Fulfillment: In the genealogy in the Gospel of Luke, Jesus is listed as being in the lineage of David. "Jesus . . . the son of David . . ." (Luke 3:23–31).

3. *Prophecy: The Messiah would be born in the city of Bethlehem.* "But as for you, Bethlehem . . . too little to be among the clans of Judah, from you One will go forth for Me to be ruler in Israel. His goings forth are from long ago, from the days of eternity" (Micah 5:2 NASB).

Fulfillment: Jesus was born in Bethlehem. "For today in the city of David (Bethlehem) there has been born for you a Savior, who is Christ the Lord" (Luke 2:11 NASB).

These prophecies have to do with the birth of Jesus, the Messiah. Other remarkable prophecies concern His death, some of them in the Old Testament, and some of them in the Gospels.

4. *Prophecy: The Messiah would be betrayed by a friend.* "Even my close friend, in whom I trusted, who ate my bread, has lifted up his heel against me" (Psalm 41:9 NASB).

Fulfillment: Jesus was betrayed by Judas Iscariot, one of His twelve disciples. ". . . Judas Iscariot, who also betrayed Him . . ." (Matthew 10:4).

5. *Prophecy: The Messiah would be tortured and crucified.* "But He was pierced through for our transgressions, He was crushed for our iniquities. The chastening for our well-being fell upon Him, and by His scourging we are healed" (Isaiah 53:5 NASB).

Fulfillment: Jesus was beaten and then crucified. "Then he (Pilate) released Barabbas for them; but after having Jesus scourged, he delivered Him to be crucified" (Matthew 27:26 NASB).

6. *Prophecy: Jesus would rise from the dead.* "For Thou wilt not abandon my soul to Sheol (the place of the departed dead); neither wilt Thou allow Thy Holy One to undergo decay" (Psalm 16:10 NASB).

Fulfillment: Jesus rose from the dead. "And the angel answered and said to the women, "Do not be afraid; for I know that you are looking for Jesus who has been crucified. He is not here, for He has risen, just as He said. Come, see the place where He was lying" (Matthew 28:5–6 NASB).

We could continue with many more prophecies and fulfillments. I have selected only a few of the major ones to give an idea of Jesus' remarkable life as it fulfilled one after another of the prophecies that told of the Messiah, in some cases, thousands of years before He was born. Again, in *Evidence that Demands a Verdict* (167), we see that the chance that any man might have lived down to the present time and fulfilled just eight of the major prophecies that Jesus fulfilled are 1 in 10 to the 17th power. That is, one in 100,000,000,000,000,000.

In order to help us comprehend these staggering odds, suppose we take this many silver dollars (10 to the 17th power) and lay them on the face of Texas. Now, as you know, Texas is a big state. If you could flip Texas west using El Paso as a hinge, Houston would land in the Pacific Ocean. If you could flip Texas east, using Houston as a hinge, El Paso would land in the Atlantic. If you could flip Texas north using the top of the panhandle as a hinge, the lowest part of Texas would land just short of the Canadian border. Texas is a big state. This many silver dollars (10 to the 17th power) would cover the entire state two feet deep in coins.

Jesus fulfilled all messianic prophecies.

Now imagine that one of those silver dollars was painted red. Blindfold a man and tell him that he can travel anywhere in the state he wants to, and pick up one silver dollar. Keep in mind that traveling at seventy miles per hour, he could not drive across Texas in a day. His chances of getting the marked silver dollar are approximately the same as a person fulfilling eight major prophecies of the Messiah by chance. Now, consider that Jesus fulfilled forty-eight prophecies. The odds that any one man fulfilled all forty-eight by chance are 10 to the 157th power. There is no practical way even to illustrate that number. Let's just say that there is about as good a chance of a tornado going through a junk yard and assembling a perfect automobile. When we look at the fulfilled prophecies in the life of Christ, the Bible becomes a very convincing book, and Jesus becomes a very convincing Messiah, God the Son.

Of course, these prophecies deal only with Jesus. But many more prophecies in the Bible were fulfilled. These are not fortune-cookie prophecies, like "an attractive person will soon come into your life," or "things will soon begin looking up for you." No, these are specific and verifiable. The Bible itself makes it clear that fulfilled prophecy attests to the supernatural origin of the word of its prophets (Jeremiah 28:9). If a prophet ever spoke anything that did not come true, he was not a true prophet (Deuteronomy 18:20–22) and was to be stoned.

The odds of these prophecies being accidentally fulfilled are virtually zero. But look at the record of the psychics in the tabloid papers. No one is able, on any level of credibility, to prophesy things that come true. Yet the Bible is full of such prophecies. They create a set of odds so remarkable that, if the prophecies are believed, they validate the Bible as the word of God. Only if you do not want to accept that conclusion do you dismiss them.

The odds of biblical prophecies being accidentally fulfilled are nearly zero.

Do Changed Lives Testify to the Truth of the Bible?

The hearts of multiplied millions of people throughout the last two thousand years have been transformed by the Bible, lending weight to its being the word of God.

Today, the explosion of Christianity, especially in places where the governments have tried to stamp it out, is a phenomenon demanding explanation. What could account for it? From the first twelve disciples until today, from the world's viewpoint, many would benefit tremendously by denying Christianity, and yet they won't. Why? Because they cannot deny the most important thing in their lives. Most of the twelve disciples died a tortured death because of their faith. They really knew what was going on with Jesus' death, burial, resurrection and post-resurrection appearances, and His ascension. Would every one of them die a dreadful death for something he knew to be a lie? They said, in essence, "Go ahead and kill me if you want to, but I know it is true." They had every reason to recant their position, but didn't.

Since the time of the apostles, thousands have followed in their footsteps. *Foxe's Book of Martyrs* presents an account of the deaths of many early Christians for their faith. The stories send a deep chill into the bones of anyone who reads them. People were sawed in half, fed to wild animals, and forced to stand unprotected in the cold until they froze to death, yet they could have escaped this by denying Jesus. This they would not do.

If this happened only in a sect here or there, as in the infamous Guyana Jonestown suicide of 1978, it would not be hard to explain. Many people have died in isolated instances for foolish causes. But this has been going on for two thousand years. Millions of people have said, in essence, "I believe the Bible to be the word of God because of the impact it has had on my life, and I am willing to die for it."

For one thing, the Bible is true to reality. For example, it commands us to be sexually pure and warns us of danger if we are not. "Flee immorality. Every other sin that a man commits is outside the body, but the immoral man sins against his own body" (1 Corinthians 6:18 NASB). When people disregard this commandment, sexually transmitted diseases such as AIDS, herpes, syphilis, gonorrhea and so forth begin to ravage the body. When a person commits sexual sin, he sins against his own body.

The Bible commands husbands to love their wives just as Christ also loved the church and gave Himself up for her, and for wives to respect their husbands (Ephesians 5:25, 33). In this way, a marriage will be preserved and flourish. If one or both spouses violate these commands, the relationship often deteriorates and is frequently destroyed.

The Bible is true to reality.

The Bible commands the laborer to work as unto the Lord, for it is the Lord Jesus whom he serves (Colossians 3:23–24), and it commands the employers to treat their employees well, knowing that the master of both employer and employee is in heaven (Ephesians 6:9). When this happens, labor relations are good, productivity is likely to be high, and the economy thrives. When these commands are disobeyed, everything in the workplace erodes.

Hundreds, and perhaps thousands, of examples demonstrate that the Bible is true to what is. The Bible possesses wisdom and an understanding of the human spirit and of circumstances. By adhering to the teachings of the Bible, one can align his life with principles that bring success; by violating them, he brings failure into his life. The Bible's being true to what is also supports the claim that the Bible is the word of God.

For another thing, people's lives have been dramatically changed as a result of becoming a Christian and following the Bible. I am one of those people. My primary reason for hesitating to become a Christian was that I had turned over new leaves in my life before, and they never stayed turned over. They always rolled back to their original position. I didn't want to "go public" as a Christian, for fear that this "new leaf" would also roll back over, and I would embarrass myself as well as God. But I plunged in anyway, asking God to prove His reality to me somehow, and I repented of my sin and invited Christ into my life. I have been in a continual state of change ever since. No matter what price I ever pay, including my own life, I will never regret becoming a Christian. My testimony is only a little whisper among a vast human chorus of testimonies accumulated for two thousand years, but the Bible transformed my life, and I believe it to be the word of God.

Conclusion

No one of these evidences proves that the Bible is the word of God. But the weight of all of them taken together enables a person to believe that the Bible is the word of God. It takes a mind prejudiced in favor of the antisupernatural not to agree that the evidence for the Bible's being the word of God is strong indeed.

Speed Bump!

Question **Q1.** Does the Bible contain errors?
Answer **A1.** The Bible as originally written was *without error.*

Q2. Are the Bible manuscripts reliable?

A2. The Bible that we have today says essentially the *same* thing that the original Bible said.

Q3. How does archaeology testify to the accuracy of the Bible?

A3. Not one archaeological find disproves accounts in the Bible and many *confirm* the historical accuracy of the Bible.

Q4. Does fulfilled prophecy testify to the identity of the Bible as the word of God?

A4. The fulfilled prophecies of the Bible lend powerful *support* to its being the word of God.

Q5. Do changed lives testify to the truth of the Bible?

A5. The hearts of multiplied millions of people throughout the last two thousand years have been *transformed* by the Bible, lending weight to its being the word of God.

Fill in the Blank

Question **Q1.** Does the Bible contain errors?
Answer **A1.** The Bible as originally written was _____.

Q2. Are the Bible manuscripts reliable?

A2. The Bible that we have today says essentially the _____ thing that the original Bible said.

Q3. How does archaeology testify to the accuracy of the Bible?

A3. Not one archaeological find disproves accounts in the Bible, and many _____ the historical accuracy of the Bible.

Q4. Does fulfilled prophecy testify to the identity of the Bible as the word of God?

A4. The fulfilled prophecies of the Bible lend powerful _____ to its being the word of God.

Q5. Do changed lives testify to the truth of the Bible?

A5. The hearts of multiplied millions of people throughout the last two thousand years have been _____ by the Bible, lending weight to its being the word of God.

For Further Thought and Discussion

1. Did you believe the Bible was the word of God before reading this chapter? If you did, why? Was it because you inherited that belief from people you trusted, or because you understood why it is reasonable to believe the Bible to be the word of God? Does this chapter add to your confidence? If so, in what ways?

2. If you did not believe the Bible was the word of God, do you now? If so, why? If not, why not?

3. Does it trouble you that there are variations in the ancient manuscripts, even though they affect no doctrine of Christianity? Why or why not?

4. Does the change in your own life add to the credibility of the Bible's being the word of God? Why or why not?

What If I Don't Believe?

If I don't believe the Bible is the word of God, the lights are out and I am in the dark. I have no moral compass with which to live, I have no meaning in this life, and no hope for life after death. I have no answers for the significant questions of life, who am I, where did I come from, what am I doing here, and where am I going? I have no reason to believe that I am anything other than an animal. I am alone in the universe. In addition, I have no credible explanation for all the things that point to the Bible's being the word of God. I must live in denial of a great body of persuasive information.

For Further Study

1. Scripture

- Matthew 5:18
- Matthew 4:1–11
- John 10:35

- 2 Peter 3:16

- Luke 24:25–27

2. Books
Several books helpful in studying this subject are listed below in general order of difficulty. If I could read only one of them, I would read the first one.

>   *Know Why You Believe,* Paul Little
>   *History and Christianity,* John Warwick Montgomery
>   *God Has Spoken,* James J. Packer

3

How Did We Get the Bible?

I was very surprised to learn that the Bible did not come to us in one lump delivery, like a package in the mail, but that it was written and compiled over time in what seemed to me to be a rather loosey-goosey fashion. After climbing Mt. Sinai as God had ordered, Moses came back down with the Ten Commandments. That is easy to understand, and is very comforting. Enshrouded in clouds, with thunder

---

In this chapter we learn that . . .

1. Through several means, God revealed to us the information He wanted us to know.
2. God supernaturally inspired the writing of the Scriptures so that the writer, in his own personality, composed and recorded without error God's revelation in the original manuscripts or letters.
3. The Holy Spirit illumines the mind of the obedient believer to understand increasingly the spiritual truth of the Scripture.
4. God sovereignly oversaw the process of the church's recognizing the books and letters which God had inspired and collecting them into one book, the Bible.

---

rolling and lightning flashing, the finger of God carved His words in stone. Moses descended the mountain carrying the tablets with God's word on them. I like that. That is a system you can have real confidence in. So why didn't someone scale some other mountain, have God give him the Bible, and come down again with it in hand? A repeat of the clouds, thunder, and lightning scenario would not be essential, but would certainly be appropriate.

God could have given us the Bible in this manner: Moses might have been handed the first five books of the Bible, and one of the prophets might have received the rest of the Old Testament. After Jesus had ascended into heaven, He could have met with one of His apostles, revealed or even written everything for him, and "poof!" we'd have the Bible. John, the last apostle to die, would have been a good candidate. He was banished to the island of Patmos. I have been to the cave where he lived, according to tradition. High up on the island, it would have been a perfect setting. One late summer evening, he would be called to the top of the island, wrapped in clouds like Moses at Sinai. He would stay up there all night, and in the early morning, the cloud would dissolve into mist as John trudged back down the island to his cave, Bible in hand.

But we didn't get the Bible the easy way. Many men wrote the Bible over a long period of time. Possibly, some of them didn't even know that they were writing Scripture when they wrote.

If men wrote the Bible, why do we think it is the word of God? How can we be sure it didn't have mistakes in it? How did they get their information? Did God dictate to them what He wanted written down? When was the Bible finally completed? Did everyone recognize right away which writings were Scripture and which ones weren't? Can we really have confidence in the Bible?

> **God could have dropped a finished Bible out of heaven. The fact that He gave it quite differently should not escape us as unimportant.**

I remember feeling a little uneasy about a process that was not quite as clear-cut as I thought it should have been. However, as my understanding of the process matured and my confidence in the sovereignty of God increased, I became comfortable with how we got our Bible. I want to share that process with you in this chapter, and hope that you will come away reassured with how we got our Bible.

How Did God Communicate His Truth to Us?

*Through several means, God revealed to us the information
He wanted us to know.*

The Bible is an amazing book. It was written

- during a period of 1500 years
- by over forty different authors ranging from farmers to kings
- in mainly two different languages

- in many different countries
- touching on hundreds of different subjects.

Yet it manifests a unity that could exist only if one author were responsible for its contents. The author of the Bible is God, who has revealed His message to humanity.

The process of God's communicating reliably to humanity involves four different aspects. *Revelation* has to do with God's unveiling of Himself and truth to humanity. *Inspiration* deals with God's overseeing the process of recording His revelation without error. *Illumination* refers to the ministry of the Holy Spirit that enables believers to properly understand Scripture. *Canonicity* refers to the process of recognizing and collecting Scripture. We look first, in this chapter, at the process of revelation.

To reveal means to "unveil." Revelation has often been defined as "God's making known to humanity that which would otherwise be unknown." However, the concept is really a little more complex than that. That definition must be understood in light of the fact that there are two different kinds of revelation. One is called general revelation and the other, specific or special revelation.

General Revelation

General revelation refers to all revelation from God apart from Christ and the Bible. That would include several things:

1. Nature. Who has not looked up into the night sky with stars glittering like so many tiny crystals on black velvet, and thought "There must be a God!" That is no accident. God intended for creation to reflect Him as any piece of art reflects the artist and draws the onlooker's mind from the creation to the creator. The beauty, order, magnitude and intricacy of nature reveals to us that there is a God (Romans 1:18–20).

2. Providence. God's intervention into the affairs of a people or a person often gives evidence of His existence. More than one person who served in Vietnam acknowledges that they should have died in Vietnam, but almost miraculously didn't. As a result, they expressed a feeling that God has spared them for some reason. In dealing with nations, God has done things to cause some nations to rise and others to fall, which gives rise to speculation about divine intervention. There are any number of fairly small things which, if they had gone differently, would have resulted in the United States' losing the Revolutionary War against England.

Because those things benefitted our side, and because one result of the victory of the colonists has been the unparalleled Christian influence of the United States on the world, we have become aware of God's providence in our national affairs (Romans 8:28).

3. Conscience. Something deep inside people inclines them to believe in the supernatural. This inner conscience speaks to us all of the existence of God. King Solomon described it when he said "[God] has put eternity in their (humanity's) hearts . . ." (Ecclesiastes 3:11). Humanity's moral nature and its inner sense of right and wrong are part of this conscience. Even though cultures differ in the acts each considers right and wrong, all cultures have a sense of right and wrong. In all cultures, no matter how primitive, a person can "violate his own conscience." Explaining this phenomenon turns our thoughts to God, since God accounts for the fact that all people possess conscience (Genesis 1:27).

Nature, providence, conscience, and the moral nature of humankind all point us to God, and constitute general revelation. This general revelation is sufficient to plant in our minds the existence of God and the concept of right and wrong, and to draw our minds toward God.

Special Revelation

Special revelation refers to revelation that has come to us through the Bible and the life of Jesus.

1. Bible. Without the Bible, we might believe in the existence of God, but we would not know who He is, what He is like, if He wants or expects anything from us, or how to get to know Him. The Bible fills in those gaps. Through the Scripture, we can understand who God is and how to develop a relationship with Him.

2. Jesus. The Bible calls Jesus the Word of God (John 1:1; Revelation 19:13), which reveals a very close connection in the mind of God the Father between the written word (the Bible) and the Living Word (Jesus). Jesus has fully revealed to us what God is like, how we can be related to Him, and what God expects of us. The Bible, God's written revelation, secures the revelation Jesus provided and transmits it to the extent any writing can to all believers who live after Jesus' earthly life. General revelation tells us that God *is*, but only special revelation is sufficient to save us (Acts 4:12).

In summary, then, we can say that God has given each person on earth enough light to know which direction leads toward God.

The written word transmits the revelation of the Living Word.
If a person turns away from God, he will never find Him. If a person walks toward God, he will eventually find Him. But in finding God, he learns that it was actually God who drew him. As C. S. Lewis said, our saying that we found God is like the mouse saying it found the cat.

How Did Fallible Men Record an Infallible Message?

God supernaturally oversaw the writing of the Scriptures so that the writer, in his own personality, composed and recorded without error God's revelation in the original manuscripts or letters.

Inspiration

When we bring up the question of the infallibility of the Bible we are opening the subject of "inspiration." This word is easily misunderstood when applied to the Bible. We commonly speak of artists having been inspired to do such a great work. Shakespeare was inspired when he wrote *Hamlet*. An inspired Beethoven penned his Fifth Symphony. Michelangelo was inspired when he painted the Sistine Chapel. Sir Laurence Olivier gave an inspired performance of *Richard III*. Luciano Pavarotti sang an inspired role in Puccini's *La Boheme*. By these uses of "inspired" we mean, simply, that they transcend the ordinary. The individual reached down within himself and produced a work that was extraordinary even for other geniuses, or even for himself.

This is *not* what is meant when we say the Bible is inspired. The word "inspired," when it is used in reference to the Bible, is a technical term meaning "God-breathed." In 2 Timothy 3:16 we read, "All Scripture is given by inspiration of

"Inspiration" applied to the Bible means that all Scripture originates from God.
God [literally, is God-breathed], and is profitable for doctrine, for reproof, for correction, for instruction in righteousness, that the man of God may be complete, thoroughly equipped for every good work."

Another key passage in understanding inspiration is 2 Peter 1:20–21, which says, ". . . no prophecy of Scripture is of any private interpretation, for prophecy never came by the will of man, but holy men of God spoke as they were moved by the Holy Spirit."

These two passages together picture Scripture as coming to us from God through men. But these men were not writing purely human documents. They were being supernaturally guided to write what God wanted written, though no evidence suggests that they were taking dictation from God or anything of the sort. Each man's own personality, background, writing style, and temperament come through. You can tell when you are reading John instead of Paul, for example. Once you get to know their styles, they are easily identifiable. Jeremiah did not write like Isaiah. God worked through human agents so that, using their own individual characteristics, they composed and recorded without error God's revelation to humanity in the words of the original manuscripts or letters.

Why I Need to Know This

I need to know this in order to have confidence in the accuracy of the Bible and respect for the authority of the Bible. I need to understand that the Bible is not merely a work of humans, but a work of God, and that I need God's help to understand it.

Other Scriptures also claim divine origin. For example, in the Old Testament, people commonly claimed to speak for God. In 2 Samuel 23:2–3, King David, as he lay dying said, "The Spirit of the LORD spoke by me, / and His word was on my tongue. / The God of Israel said, / The Rock of Israel spoke to me: / 'He who rules over men must be just, / Ruling in the fear of God.' " The prophet Jeremiah said, "Then the LORD put forth His hand and touched my mouth, and the LORD said to me: 'Behold I have put My words in your mouth' " (Jeremiah 1:9–10).

When New Testament writers refer to portions of the Old Testament—their Scripture (because the New Testament was not yet written and distributed)—they uniformly treat Scripture as nothing less than God's word. And one key text in the New Testament, 2 Peter 3:16, identifies Paul's writings, which were later gathered into our New Testament, as Scripture. Peter says that Paul's epistles contain "some things hard to understand, which untaught and unstable people twist to their own destruction, as they do also the rest of the Scriptures." Thus wherever one part of our Bible refers to another, the reference either directly says that this or that portion is Scripture, that is, God's word, or the reference uses the other portion in a manner fully consistent with the teaching of 2 Timothy 3:16—that all of Scripture originates with God.

Inerrancy

Not everyone understands the same thing when we say that God's word is inspired and without error. Some say that the Bible *contains* God's word, but that the Bible has error in it, and the parts that have error are not God's word. This presents a mountain too high to climb—namely, that someone has to decide which parts of the Bible have errors and which do not. Years ago, W. A. Criswell, former pastor of First Baptist Church of Dallas, Texas, summarized this theory this way: The Bible is inspired in spots and we're inspired to pick out the spots. I agree with his conclusion, namely, that this is not acceptable. I don't trust even myself to make those decisions, let alone anyone else. When you start saying that some parts of the Bible are inspired by God and therefore without error, but other parts have error and are therefore not inspired, you step onto a slippery slope. No two people are going to agree on which parts are inspired and inerrant and which parts aren't. You end up jeopardizing the Bible altogether. It is like letting a snake get just its head through a hole. If it can get its head through, there is nothing to keep the *rest* of the snake from going through.

Therefore, we have to arrive at a definition as airtight as we can make it. *The Bible is verbally and totally inspired and without error in the original writings.* That means the individual words, not just the concepts, are inspired and without error. That also means that all the words, not just some of them, are inspired and without error. All Scripture originates in God, who is true and faithful and fully capable of communicating truth without error to human writers, which He has done through inspiring Scripture. We have multiple testimony to assure us of this truth: the testimony of Scripture about itself, which we have just discussed; the testimony of the Holy Spirit dwelling within every true believer; the testimony of countless believers who have relied upon Scripture for guidance and salvation; and the testimony of devout and careful Bible scholars who have studied Scripture and refuted the claims of some that Scripture contains error. Among such scholars, the testimony of Berkeley and Alvera M. Mickelsen is typical:

After examining thousands of passages of Scripture, [we] have concluded that the Bible teaches truth on all subjects it addresses in the ways and manners of expressing truth in ancient times. The Scriptures also illustrate truth by showing that error (idolatry, deceit, falsehood, and all forms of moral evil) brings tragedy (*Understanding Scripture* 28).

Together these testimonies assure us that the Bible, as God's written word, is nothing less than pure truth.

How Can Humans Understand Divine Information?

The Holy Spirit illumines the mind of the obedient believer to understand increasingly the spiritual truth of the Scripture.

Illumination

Several passages of Scripture help us arrive at our understanding of the illumining ministry of the Holy Spirit. John 16:12–15 says:

> I have many more things to say to you, but you cannot bear them now. But when He, the Spirit of truth, comes, He will guide you into all the truth; for He will not speak on His own initiative, but whatever He hears, He will speak; and He will disclose to you what is to come. He shall glorify Me; for He shall take of Mine, and shall disclose it to you. All things that the Father has are Mine; therefore I said, that He takes of Mine, and will disclose it to you (NASB).

We add to Jesus' words the writings of the apostle Paul in 1 Corinthians 2:9—3:3:

> As it is written, "things which eye has not seen and ear has not heard, and which have not entered the heart of man, all that God has prepared for those who love him." For to us God revealed them through the Spirit; for the Spirit searches all things, even the depths of God. For who among men knows the thoughts of a man except the spirit of the man, which is in him? Even so the thoughts of God no one knows except the Spirit of God.
>
> Now we have received, not the spirit of the world, but the Spirit who is from God, that we might know the things freely given to us by God, which things we also speak, not in words taught by human wisdom, but in those taught by the Spirit, combining spiritual thoughts with spiritual words. But a natural man does not accept the things of the Spirit of God; for they are fool-

ishness to him, and he cannot understand them, because they are
spiritually appraised.

But he who is spiritual appraises all things, yet he himself is
appraised by no man. For who has known the mind of the Lord,
that he should instruct him? But we have the mind of Christ. And
I, brethren, could not speak to you as to spiritual men, but as to
men of flesh, as to babes in Christ. I gave you milk to drink, not
solid food; for you were not yet able to receive it. Indeed, even
now you are not yet able, for you are still fleshly (NASB).

Finally, we read the words of the apostle John:

And as for you, the anointing which you received from Him
abides in you, and you have no need for anyone to teach you; but
as His anointing teaches you about all things, and is true and is
not a lie, and just as it has taught you, you abide in Him (1 John
2:27).

From these passages, we learn several things:

1. The Holy Spirit helps the Christian understand the spiritual things of the Bible.
2. The more spiritually mature a Christian is, the more he can
   understand.
3. Nothing can substitute for this ministry. The truth may be
   grasped only by the illuminating ministry of the Spirit.

Certainly, the "natural man," the non-Christian, can understand some things of the Bible. For example, when it says that
Jesus walked from Bethany to Jerusalem, the natural man is as capable of understanding that as the Christian. But when it comes
to the spiritual truths, what Paul called "the things freely given to
us by God . . . those [words] taught by the Spirit, combining spiritual {thoughts} with spiritual words"—these things can only be
understood by the Christian.

How Was the Bible Finally Compiled?

*God sovereignly oversaw the process of the church's recognizing the
books and letters which God had inspired and collecting them into one
book, the Bible.*

Canonicity

If the Bible did not come down to us in a completed package
from a storm-topped mountain, where did the actual book

come from? How did we get it? How did we get what is called the "canon?" (Canon means "accepted as genuine writings.") So the question is, how was it determined what books were accepted as Scripture and included in the Bible. The question must be answered for the Old Testament first, and then the New Testament.

Old Testament Canon

First, an important point must be made. A letter or manuscript belonged in the Old Testament canon if it was inspired by God. The trick is, how was it decided whether or not a given letter or manuscript was inspired by God? That question is the same for both the Old and New Testaments, but the answers are somewhat different. For the Old Testament, it is not clear to us on what grounds the authority of a writing was accepted. That it was accepted, however, is clear. Jesus Himself stamped His approval on the thirty-nine books which make up our Old Testament. In Luke 11:51, Jesus rebukes the hypocritical religious leaders of His time. He was pronouncing a series of "woes" on them for their attitudes and actions. "Woe to you Pharisees! For you love the best seats in the synagogues and greetings in the marketplaces. Woe to you, scribes and Pharisees, hypocrites! For you are like graves which are not seen, and the men who walk over them are not aware of them!" And so on.

He pronounced one "woe" on them because they had shed the blood of the prophets "from the blood of Abel to the blood of Zechariah . . ." This statement makes sense when we understand how the Hebrew Bible and the Old Testament of our English Bible are organized differently. In the Hebrew Bible, Genesis is the first book and 2 Chronicles, instead of Malachi, is the last. Abel is found in the first book of the Hebrew Bible, Genesis. Zechariah is found in the last book of the Hebrew Bible, 2 Chronicles. When Jesus blasts them for shedding the blood of the first prophet to the last prophet and all prophets in between, He is really saying, "Your guilt is recorded through the entire Bible, from Genesis to 2 Chronicles!" From beginning to end!

> **Jesus Himself stamped His approval on the thirty-nine books that make up our Bible.**

Some people claim that all the books of the Old Testament canon were recognized and collected into one volume by Ezra in the fifth century B.C. References by the Jewish historian Josephus, whose life overlapped that of the apostles, indicate that the thirty-nine books which we recognize today as the Old Testament were recognized as Scripture then. Other facts support this conclusion, giving us good reason to believe that all the books of our Old Testament were accepted by devout Jews as Scripture by the time of Jesus.

New Testament Canon

How the New Testament books were recognized and collected into one volume is somewhat clearer. Again, we restate that books were Scripture because they were inspired by God. However, God did not give us a list of the inspired books to be collected into the New Testament. In His sovereignty, He oversaw that process from heaven.

Many of the New Testament books were written by apostles. Paul and Peter clearly wrote with their apostolic authority in mind. Peter specifically refers to Paul's letters as Scripture:

. . . our beloved brother Paul, according to the wisdom given to him, has written to you, as also in all his [letters], speaking in them of these things, in which are some things hard to understand, which are untaught and unstable people twist to their own destruction, as they do also the rest of the Scriptures (2 Peter 3:15–16).

One criterion of inspiration was whether or not the document was written by an apostle. Though not apostles, Mark and Luke carried great weight because they were such close associates of the apostles. A second criterion was whether or not they were recognized as authoritative by the early church. This criterion is important because, as books were written during the lifetime of the apostles, the apostles could easily have aided in the process of recognizing inspired writings, and once their approval was given to a letter or book, that approval was passed down through church tradition. A third criterion was whether or not the letter or book conformed to the high standards set by other books that were already recognized as Scripture.

Although God inspired each New Testament book, He did not give us a list of the books to be included.

The result of this process was that the books we have in our Old and New Testaments were officially acknowledged as Scripture by the Council of Carthage, a gathering of church leaders in A.D. 397, around three hundred years after the death of the last apostle, John. Since that time, the thirty-nine Old Testament books and the twenty-seven New Testament books have formed the canon of Scripture for all Christians, a list that for Protestant believers remains unchanged today.

While it is interesting and helpful to know about the formation of the canon of Scriptural books and letters, we must rest on the sovereignty of God for their authenticity. If God is going to hold us accountable to truth, He must see to it that we have the truth. God, in His providence, oversaw the process of forming the canon. The witness of the Spirit in the hearts of believers who read the books of the Scriptures, and the change which the Holy Spirit brings about in their lives, is a final telling testimony to the fact that we have the Word of God as He intended.

Speed Bump!

Question **A**nswer

Q1. How did God communicate His truth to us?

A1. Through several means, God *revealed* to us the information He wanted us to know.

Q2. How did fallible men record an infallible message?

A2. God supernaturally inspired the writing of the Scriptures so that the writer, in his own personality, composed and recorded without error God's revelation in the original manuscripts or letters.

Q3. How can humans understand divine information?

A3. The Holy Spirit *illumines* the mind of the obedient believer to understand increasingly the spiritual truth of the Scripture.

Q4. How was the Bible finally compiled?

A4. God sovereignly *oversaw* the process of the church's recognizing the books and letters which God had inspired and collecting them into one book, the Bible.

Fill in the Blank

Question **A**nswer

Q1. How did God communicate His truth to us?

A1. Through several means, God _____ to us the information He wanted us to know.

Q2. How did fallible men record an infallible message?

A2. God supernaturally _____ the writing of the Scriptures so that the writer, in his own personality, composed and recorded without error God's revelation in the original manuscripts or letters.

Q3. How can humans understand divine information?

A3. The Holy Spirit _____ the mind of the obedient believer to understand increasingly the spiritual truth of the Scripture.

Q4. How was the Bible finally compiled?

A4. God sovereignly _____ the process of the church's recognizing the books and letters which God had inspired and collecting them into one book, the Bible.

For Further Thought and Discussion

1. Describe in your own words your understanding of the difference between Shakespeare's having been inspired to write *Hamlet* and Paul's having been inspired to write Romans.

2. Have you ever had an experience in which you suddenly understood in a fresher or deeper way a passage of Scripture which you had known for a long time? How would you explain that experience, based on the information in this chapter?

3. What role do you think obedience plays in understanding Scripture?

4. Do you have confidence that the Bible we have is the Bible God wanted us to have? Why or why not?

What If I Don't Believe?

If I don't believe this information, I will have little confidence in or respect for the Bible. I will consider the Bible only a work of humans, and am not likely to use it to guide me in all my life decisions. I will probably not understand the Bible well, because I probably will not study it diligently or depend on and pray for the Holy Spirit to open my eyes to the truth of Scripture. I will not respect the church, since the church is founded on the Scriptures as the word of God. My ability to fellowship with Christians who do believe this information will be limited. It would be very difficult for me to be a Christian without believing the Bible. Much is at stake.

For Further Study

1. Scripture

- Matthew 5:18

- Luke 24:25–27

- 1 Timothy 3:16–17

- Hebrews 4:12

- 2 Peter 1:21

- 2 Peter 3:15–16

2. Books

Other books helpful in studying this subject are listed below in general order of difficulty. If I could read only one of them, I would read the first one.

> *Know Why You Believe,* Paul Little
> *History and Christianity,* John Warwick Montgomery
> *A Survey of Bible Doctrine,* Charles Ryrie
> *Evidence that Demands a Verdict,* Josh McDowell

I have but this to say, the Bible is the best gift God has given to man. All the good the Savior gave to the world was communicated through this book. But for it we could not know right from wrong. All things most desirable for man's welfare, here and hereafter, are to be found portrayed in it.
■ Abraham Lincoln

4

How Has the Bible Been Viewed Historically?

Twenty years ago, I attended a banquet at which W. A. Criswell, the venerable former pastor of First Baptist Church in Dallas, Texas, gave the keynote speech. He told a story of the time he came to Fort Worth from Oklahoma to attend seminary. An eager young preacher-to-be, he had earlier prayed under a large live oak tree in Oklahoma for God to use him mightily in ministry. He prayed, "Oh, God, give me a church. Give me a big church. Oh, God, give me a church of at least two hundred." That is comical today, because when he retired from the pastorate of First Baptist Church, its membership probably numbered over twenty-five thousand.

Fresh off his experience of pleading to God to be used mightily in the ministry, Criswell went to seminary in Fort Worth, and on one of his first Sundays there found himself in a Unitarian church. The pastor preached on Shakespeare. After the service, Criswell went up to the pastor and said, "Pardon me, sir, but I thought that in a church, we ought to preach the Bible, not Shakespeare." The Unitarian pastor replied, "Oh, I preach the Bible. In fact, I preached the Bible last year, but I finished with it, and so this year, I'm preaching Shakespeare!"

Criswell said that rudely awakened him to the knowledge that not everyone viewed the Bible as he did—the word of God, and inexhaustible by humanity. I confess, it was a rather rude awakening to me, too. Why would anyone bother with any form of religion if he didn't believe the Bible? If I didn't believe the Bible, I would follow the biblical admonition to "eat, drink and be merry, for tomorrow, we die." Of course, different people pursue pleasure in various ways, but one thing I know I wouldn't be doing. I wouldn't be wasting my time preaching Shakespeare to people on Sunday morning!

This raises the question of how different people view the Bible. My early days as a Christian were somewhat sheltered, and I assumed that all Christians viewed the Bible the same way I did. After a few years of formal theological education and some jarring personal experiences, I learned how naive I had been. In this chapter, then, we will look at several ways the Bible has been viewed historically.

How Has the Bible Been Viewed by Those Who Reject Christianity?

Some view the Bible solely as a product of human insight, and reject it as being the word of God.

Actually, three main groups of people fill this category. First are atheists. They believe that they know enough to know that there is no God. Ironically, no one could know that for sure unless he were omniscient (all-knowing), a supernatural ability. Would the atheist then be god? That logical inconsistency aside, atheists believe that the Bible is a book of human insight, wisdom, and experience, but is no more divine in origin than Shakespeare, Plato, or Socrates. They consider the evidence supporting the divine origin of Scripture untrustworthy or inconclusive. Atheists will admit that a great deal of practical wisdom can be found in the Bible, and that by following it life on earth can be improved (such as doing unto others as you would have others do unto you—the Golden Rule). Beyond that, the book has no credibility with them. Fulfilled prophecies are fabrications or coincidences. Divine claims are worthless since anyone can claim divine authority. The resurrection is a hoax or a mystery, and not capable of lending Scripture any credibility. This is no surprise, of course. What else would we expect of atheists? Those who accept the message of the Bible cannot be atheists.

The second group of people, agnostics, say that they don't know if the Bible is the word of God. They stop short of saying that it isn't. They say it is not possible to know, or at least not possible for them to know, if the Bible is the word of God. It might be, but it might not be. However, rather than to err on the side of safety, agnostics fall short of treating it as a divine document.

Frankly, so much is at stake that even if I only thought the Bible might be the word of God, I would follow it just to be sure. I'm not much of a gambler.

Unlike the atheist and agnostic, the third kind of person who rejects Christianity has adopted a religion based on another body of religious writing. For example, a Muslim has his own religious book, the Koran, which cannot be true if the Bible is true. You must choose between them, because the books contradict each other. For example, since the prophet Muhammad, the founder of Islam, was not born until A.D. 570, Muslims consider Abraham, Jonah, Moses, and Jesus to be prophets of God, and all their writings as scripture until the final revelation (the Koran) of the last prophet, Muhammad. Anyone who does not accept the teachings of the Koran as the final authority merely proves that he is not a sincere follower of Allah (God). Therefore, Jesus was merely a prophet, and not to be followed as the ultimate authority. Jesus made a similar claim years before Muhammad ever came on the scene. He said, "I am the way, the truth and the life. No one comes to the Father except through Me" (John 14:6). So there you have it. One must choose between Jesus and Muhammad.

Similar circumstances exist with all other established and organized religions. If you are a Buddhist, you cannot be a Christian. If you are a Hindu, you cannot be a Christian. If you are a Confucianist, you cannot be a Christian. Therefore, followers of other religions, as well as agnostics and atheists, do not view the Bible as the exclusive, authoritative word of God.

How Has the Bible Been Viewed by Those Who Think That Part but not All of the Bible is the Word of God?

Some people believe that, while not all the Bible is the word of God, the Bible contains the word of God.

Two camps of people believe that the Bible may not be the word of God, but that it contains the word of God. Those in the first camp have studied or been influenced by what is called "higher criticism" or the "historical-critical" method so that they do not believe in the miraculous power of God. This discipline goes back about two hundred years to Germany, where scholars began their study of the Bible without assuming it was different from any other literature. The leader seems to have been a professor, Johann Salomo Semler, who taught at the University of Halle. Harold Lindsell, in his book, *God's Incomparable Word*, outlines the historical development of this line of thought. Apparently, Semler did not believe in the divine inspiration of the Bible; he rejected miracles and the supernatural in general. Therefore, anything in the Bible that included miracles and the supernatural had to be explained. He explained them by saying that matters relating to faith were the word of God, but matters relating to history or science were not the word of God, and filled with errors. As Semler would have put it, the Bible is not the word of God, but it contains the word of God.

The most important question about the Bible is, Do you believe God has communicated to us in a reliable way?

Therefore, the task of many scholars for the last two hundred years has been to find the word of God within the Bible. This poses an impossibility, however, because no two people agree on what is the word of God and what are merely the writings of men. No two modern critics have ever come up with exactly the same answers as to what is the word of God and what is not: Each person must discover the word of God for himself as he reads. As a result, preachers cannot preach the Bible as the authoritative word of God. They cannot say, "God says," because someone in the congregation can say, "well, you may think God said that, but I don't think He did! And why should I accept your conclusions if I don't agree with you?"

At its heart, it is a philosophical and theological problem. By that I mean that you cannot prove your point no matter what position you take. If you say all the Bible is the word of God, or if you say that only part of the Bible is the word of God, you cannot prove your position. The question is, do you believe that God has communicated to us in a reliable way or not? Do you believe that God performs miracles or not? (What good is a God if He cannot perform miracles?) Do you believe that God would leave us to our own ability to "reason out" what is the word of God and what is not? Humanity's ability to reason should give anyone some major doubts.

Life becomes subjective guesswork unless all the Bible is the word of God. Recently, a group of seventy scholars got together and voted on what part of the Gospels were said by Jesus, and what parts were added by writers who attributed things to Jesus that He did not really say. That is what we are reduced to: voting, or just deciding on our own, what is the word of God and what isn't.

Several specific problems are worth noting. First, as has been shown, the Bible becomes a subjective book, vulnerable to the whims of whoever reads it.

In this chapter we learn that . . .

1. Some view the Bible solely as a product of human insight and reject it as being the word of God.
2. Some people believe that, while not all the Bible is the word of God, the Bible contains the word of God.
3. Although areas of the Bible have been historically contested, all Christians have historically agreed on a large body of truth.

Second, people who hold to this position often say that the Bible has errors in it in the areas of history and science, but that it is accurate in matters of faith and practice. The problem is that often matters of history science are intertwined with matters of faith and practice. Take the Resurrection, for example. History and science would tell you that the Resurrection could not have happened. But the Bible says that it did. Jesus said that it did. His disciples said that it did. We are exhorted to live in hope that when we die, we will be resurrected just as Jesus was. We are encouraged to take strength in this life, knowing that in the next life we will be delivered from all pain, suffering, and sorrow. If Jesus didn't rise from the dead, we can take no hope in such things. We cannot draw strength from them. We have no reason to follow Jesus' example in suffering. Paul said that if the resurrection is not true then our faith is in vain, the apostles are liars, and we are to be pitied above all other people (1 Corinthians 15:14–19). History and faith issues are so interwoven that we cannot separate them. The whole fabric becomes unraveled when we start pulling threads.

Matters of history and of faith are so intertwined that they can't be separated.

Ethics also collapse. If Paul is wrong in a given ethical teaching, as many modern scholars claim he is, why is he not wrong on other ethical teachings? Therefore, "right" and "wrong" disappear. You cannot use the words right and wrong anymore, because no one can say authoritatively what is right and wrong. Too much of the foundation for determining right and wrong from the Scripture has been eroded. We fall into situation ethics, subjectivity reigns supreme, and any basis for objectivity is lost.

Lindsell writes:

Years ago, Bishop G. Bromley Oxnam of the Methodist Church said that God never ordered the slaughter of the Midianites and any God who did this is a "Dirty Bully." Yet the Scripture says God did just that, and claims that God is holy, just and righteous.

Still others say that God did not and could not have ordered Abraham to offer up Isaac as a burnt offering on Mt. Moriah. What does all of this mean?

In every case, it means that people who hold these views reject what the Scriptures assert. They do it, not on the basis of Scripture, but on the basis of so-called evidence outside the Scripture that is used to judge Scripture. Or they do it because it is their subjective opinion that what happened is not credible. Now if what these critics assert is true, then at least these parts of the Bible are untrue. And what is untrue cannot be the word of God (*God's Incomparable Word* 91).

When Scripture contradicts Scripture, then the Bible as the word of God has been destroyed, and subjectivity is the only principle of decision-making.

The second camp that believes the Bible may not be the word of God, but that it contains the word of God, are people who believe that all truth is relative. Close philosophical cousins of the people we have been talking about, they say, "Since all truth is relative, what may be true for you may not be true for me. But if it is true for you, go for it." These people would not challenge anyone who said that he found truth in the Bible. They would just say, "Don't try to force your truth on us." Under these circumstances, these "relativists" would not argue with someone "finding the word of God in the Bible," but they would never agree that the whole Bible is the word of God, because then they would fall under the condemnation of God for not accepting Jesus.

If the Bible merely contains God's word, who is authorized to say what is God's and what is merely human?

How Has the Bible Been Viewed by Those Who Accept Christianity and the Bible as the Word of God?

Although areas of the Bible have been historically contested, all Christians have historically agreed on a large body of truth.

If we say that, today, we believe the Scriptures to be inspired, authoritative, and trustworthy, it would be odd indeed if we found that no one through the centuries held this view. Why should we believe it if no one else has, especially those who lived close to the time of the writing of the Scriptures? But if the church throughout its history believed the Bible to be inspired, authoritative, and trustworthy, then that belief would be yet another pillar of support for the Bible. Our task, then, is to consider how the church, from earliest times to the present, has regarded the Bible.

The Old Testament scholars of Jesus' day, as well as Jesus, held the highest view of the Old Testament. Jesus Himself said:

Throughout history, the church has uniformly claimed the Bible's total truthfulness.

Do not think that I came to abolish the Law or the Prophets; I did not come to abolish, but to fulfill. For truly I say to you, until heaven and earth pass away, not the smallest letter or stroke shall pass away from the Law, until all is accomplished. Whoever then annuls one of the least of these commandments, and so teaches others, shall be called least in the kingdom of heaven; but whoever keeps and teaches them, he shall be called great in the kingdom of heaven (Matthew 5:17–19 NASB).

Never in any of Jesus' dealings with religious leaders did anyone question the authority and integrity of the Old Testament. Throughout the Bible, it is taken for granted that the Scriptures are the work of divine inspiration, and therefore inerrant, authoritative, and infallible. The Scripture must be "accomplished" we read in Luke 22:37. What was written there was "written for our instruction," we read in Romans 15:4 and 1 Corinthians 10:11. Neither Jesus, nor a religious leader of His time, nor a New Testament writer would ever dream of questioning a statement contained in the Old Testament, though the exact manner or mode of its inspiration was not explained in the Old Testament. In the

New Testament, Paul clearly stated in 2 Timothy 3:16–17, that "all Scripture is inspired by God and profitable for teaching, for reproof, for correction, for training in righteousness; that the man of God may be adequate, equipped for every good work" (NASB). This surely applied, in Paul's mind, to the Old Testament Scriptures, but may also have applied to New Testament Scripture, since the apostles seemed to be aware that things were being written in their day that were to be considered Scripture (2 Peter 3:16).

Not until the historical-critical method emerged from Europe about two hundred years ago did anyone question the inspiration, inerrancy, infallibility, and authority of Scripture. Until that time, the Scriptures were regarded as writings of the Holy Spirit, with no room left for the possibility that human hands might have messed up the intention of God. The historic view is that the writers were used by God as a workman uses his tools; the actual words, rather than the writers, were considered inspired. All the orthodox early church fathers reflected this viewpoint. Augustine, one of the greatest of the church fathers, and one who had tremendous influence on Calvin, wrote, "The Faith will totter if the authority of the Holy Scriptures loses its hold on men. We must surrender ourselves to the authority of the Holy Scripture, for it can neither mislead nor be misled." He went on to say that once you admit a single error in the Bible you open the door to a floodtide of unbelief,

Augustine denied that anything false is found in Scripture.

> for it seems to me that most disastrous consequences must follow upon our believing that anything false is found in the sacred books: that is to say, that the men by whom the Scripture has been given to us, and committed to writing, did put down in these books anything false. It is one question whether it may be at any time the duty of a good man to deceive; but it is another question whether it can have been the duty of a writer of Holy Scripture to deceive: nay, it is not another question—it is no question at all. For if you once admit into such a high sanctuary of authority one false statement as made in the way of duty, there will not be left a single sentence of those books which, if appearing to any one difficult in practice or hard to believe, may not by the same fatal rule be explained away, as a statement in which, intentionally, and

under a sense of duty, the author declared what was not true (in Lindsell 54–55).

Martin Luther, the leader of the Reformation in the 1500s, wrote, "This I have learned to do: to hold only those books which

---

Why I Need to Know This

If I don't know this, I can be led astray by what others who don't believe the Bible say. If I know the areas of disagreement ahead of time, I am not shaken when I learn of churched people who attack the integrity of the Bible as the word of God. I can also rest in the fact that, while many true Christians disagree about certain areas of the Bible, there is, nevertheless, a larger body of information about which all Christians have agreed, and this body of agreement contains information crucial to the Bible.

---

are called the Holy Scriptures in such honor that I finally believe that not one of the holy writers ever erred." This has been the historic position of the Catholic church as well (Lindsell 58).

Finally, we turn our attention to the witness of the various denominations and theological persuasions regarding the trustworthiness of the Bible. An excellent summary of these witnesses is found in Lindsell's book, and I draw on his fine work to summarize some well-known positions.

Numerous historic confessions affirm the complete inspiration and truthfulness of Scripture.

The Westminster Confession of Faith. This confession, championed most conspicuously by Presbyterians, in chapter one calls the Scripture the "only infallible rule of faith and practice."

The Belgic Confession. This confession is advocated by the Reformed Church in America. In article 4 of the confession, we read:

We receive these books (the sixty-six books of the Old and New Testament), and only these books as holy and canonical, for the regulation, foundation, and confirmation of our faith; believing without any doubt all things contained in them, not so much because the Church receives and approves them as such, but more especially because the Holy Ghost witnesseth in our hearts that they are from God, whereof they carry the evidence in themselves. For the very blind are able to perceive that the things foretold in them are fulfilling.

The New Hampshire Confession. This is a Baptist confession:

> We believe that the Holy Bible was written by men divinely inspired, and is a perfect treasure of heavenly instruction: that it has God for its author, salvation for its end, and truth without any mixture of error, for its matter; that it reveals the principles by which God will judge us; and therefore is, and shall remain to the end of the world, the true center of Christian union, and the supreme standard by which all human conduct, creeds, and opinions should be tried.

Lutheran Confessions. All the historic Lutheran confessions testify to the inspired, inerrant, infallible trustworthiness of the Bible. Worthy of special mention is the America Lutheran Church, Evangelical Lutheran Church, the Lutheran Church— Missouri Synod, and the Wisconsin Evangelical Lutheran Synod.

Anglicans, Methodists, and Episcopalians. Though great diversity among these traditions exists today, the founding documents of these denominations include clear statements of belief in the inspiration, inerrancy, infallibility and trustworthiness of the Bible.

There are devout and learned Christians who would wholeheartedly affirm the Bible's trustworthiness but would not affirm inerrancy as I have qualified it here. I do not want to question their spiritual integrity; however, when I look not only at the evidence, but also at the impossible situation which it seems to me is created when humans have to decide what is the word of God and what is not, I deem it necessary to take a strict view of the subject. It seems to me that, in the end, a person gives up the possibility of knowing anything for sure if he gives up on the inerrancy of the Bible.

When I look at the facts, it would take a courageous act for me to question not only scriptural statements, but also the church traditions from the very beginning until today. I believe the Bible is the word of God. All of it. The original writings do not err in matters spiritual, historical, or scientific. They teach truth on all subjects they address in the ways and manners of expressing truth in ancient times. The Bible is God's revealed word to humankind for salvation and spiritual life.

Speed Bump!

Question **A**nswer

Q1. How has the Bible been viewed by those who reject Christianity?

A1. Some view the Bible solely as a product of *human* insight, and reject it as being the word of God.

Q2. How has the Bible been viewed by those who think that part but not all of the Bible is the word of God?

A2. Some people believe that, while not all the Bible is the word of God, the Bible *contains* the word of God.

Q3. How has the Bible been viewed by those who accept Christianity and the Bible as the word of God?

A3. Although areas of the Bible have been historically contested, all Christians have historically *agreed* on a large body of truth.

Fill in the Blank

Question **A**nswer

Q1. How has the Bible been viewed by those who reject Christianity?

A1. Some view the Bible solely as a product of _____ insight, and reject it as being the word of God.

Q2. How has the Bible been viewed by those who think that part but not all of the Bible is the word of God?

A2. Some people believe that, while not all the Bible is the word of God, the Bible _____ the word of God.

Q3. How has the Bible been viewed by those who accept Christianity and the Bible as the word of God?

A3. Although areas of the Bible have been historically contested, all Christians have historically _____ on a large body of truth.

For Further Thought and Discussion

1. Have you ever thought about the distinction between the Bible *being* the word of God and the Bible's *containing* the word of God? What, in your own words, is the importance of the distinction?

2. Why do you think people would reject the Bible as the word of God, and yet stay in "religious" or "Christian" activity? Would you?

3. What degree of comfort or assurance does it give you to know that all major church denominations from the earliest days of the church have agreed on the trustworthiness of the Bible? How much credibility does that carry with you?

What If I Don't Believe?

If I don't believe in the trustworthiness of the Bible, I do not have a reliable picture of God, I do not have a sound understanding of what He asks of me and promises me, and I have no well-founded hope of life after death.

For Further Study

1. Scripture

- 2 Peter 1:19–21
- 2 Timothy 3:16–17
- Matthew 5:17–19
- Revelation 22:18–19

2. Books
Other books helpful in studying this subject are listed below in general order of difficulty. If I could read only one of them, I would read the first one.

> *Know Why You Believe*, Paul Little
> *A Survey of Bible Doctrine*, Charles Ryrie
> *God's Incomparable Word*, Harold Lindsell

Hammer away, ye hostile hands,
Your hammers break; God's anvil stands.
■ inscription on a monument to the
Huguenots at Paris

What Is the Story
of the Old Testament?

Lady was an amazing dog, a border collie with that innate instinct to herd animals and control anything that moved. White collared her black body and streaked her dark muzzle. A perfect physical specimen, with keen eyes, sharp ears, brilliant mind, and inexhaustible body, Lady worked the farm animals as I was growing up. The love of her life was to bring in the cows when they needed to be milked. Her internal clock told her when it was time to round up the cows, but the cows had an internal clock too, and they would come in by themselves. However, Lady would miss her fun if they came up on their own. So, she sized up the situation, set her clock ahead, and herded them in a half-hour before milking time.

Her second great love was capturing wayward pigs. Pigs can be very difficult to handle because they are so smart, and they have their own agenda for what they want to do. When pigs get out of their pens, they can be notoriously difficult to get back in. This gave Lady the opportunity to herd, run, chase, and bite with wild abandon. What fun!

Her most fruitless habit was nipping the tires on the tractor. For some reason, the great, black, rotating treads seemed to threaten her control of circumstances, and she dedicated herself, with maniacal zeal, to biting the treads of the tractor tires to get them to stop. I tried repeatedly and sternly to get her to stop this deadly game, but to no avail. She never lost the game, thank goodness.

When it comes to studying and understanding the Bible, many of us feel our efforts are as futile as Lady's biting the tractor tires. The Bible is so much bigger and so much more powerful than we are that the thought of mastering the Bible overwhelms us. Shortly after I became a Christian, I decided to read the Bible from beginning to end, and get it under my belt. I only knew snatches of the Bible—amazing stories here, poignant parables there, a few touching verses somewhere else. But I lacked a comprehensive view of it. Not seeing the big picture limited my ability to understand all the little pictures I saw in the Bible. So I tackled it, sort of like Lady's attacking the tractor tires. But unlike Lady, I admitted defeat rather quickly. Then, I learned several key elements which helped me find my way around in the Bible and understand it more completely. One of those keys was understanding how the books of the Old Testament divided the story into segments. We'll look at that key in this chapter.

What Is the Capsule Summary of the Old Testament?

The Old Testament is primarily the story of God's dealings with humanity through the nation of Israel.

The most basic story line of the Old Testament is fairly simple. God created Adam and Eve, who sinned and were driven out of the Garden of Eden. As their offspring multiplied into the millions, so sin multiplied. Humanity became so sinful that God destroyed the earth with a universal flood, preserving Noah and his immediate family to repopulate the earth with a righteous family. Sin kept its grip on humanity, however, and once again people forgot God.

Many years later, God revealed Himself to Abraham and promised Abraham a nation, many descendants, and a blessing that would extend to everyone on the earth. In believing God, Abraham became the father of a great people, the Hebrews, who were later known as the Jews. God's promises to Abraham were passed down through Isaac, Abraham's son, and Jacob, Abraham's grandson, and all twelve of Jacob's sons. From the twelve sons of Jacob descended the twelve tribes of Israel, who make up the Hebrew people.

A famine hit the land of Canaan (the same area, approximately, as the modern nation of Israel) where the Israelites were living, and they moved to Egypt to get food. In time, they became a threat to the Egyptian people because they multiplied so rapidly, so the Egyptians enslaved the Hebrew people for nearly 400 years. Finally, in response to their cries for deliverance from slavery, God raised up Moses to lead them out of Egypt back into the promised land of Canaan.

The Israelites, as they were then called, lived in the promised land in a loose governmental system for the next 400 years. Then a monarchy was established, and numerous kings ruled the Hebrews for the next four hundred years. The first 120 years of the monarchy, three famous kings each reigned forty years: Saul, David, and Solomon. Then as a result of civil conflict over taxation, the northern part of the nation seceded from the monarchy and established their own independent kingdom called Israel. The southern kingdom adopted the name of Judah.

Shortly thereafter, Assyria, a nation to the northeast, came and conquered the northern kingdom, Israel, and scattered many of them to the far corners of that part of the world. About one hundred years later, Babylonia invaded and conquered Assyria, as well as the southern kingdom of Judah, destroying Jerusalem and leading thousands of people into captivity in Babylonia.

In this chapter we learn that . . .

1. The Old Testament is primarily the story of God's dealings with humanity through the nation of Israel.
2. The entire story of the Old Testament can be broken into nine major time periods.
3. The geographical focus of the Israelites moved from Ur (where Abraham first lived), to Canaan (patriarchs), to Egypt (slavery), back to Canaan (which became Israel under the monarchy), to Babylonia (captivity), and back to Jerusalem (return).

About seventy years later, Persia defeated Babylonia to rule the entire part of the world from the western shore of the Mediterranean clear to India. The king of Persia allowed the Israelites living in captivity in Babylonia to return to Jerusalem to rebuild it. Fifty thousand people returned under the leadership of three men: Zerubbabel, Ezra, and Nehemiah. They rebuilt the city and the temple and restored public worship of God. They lived that way for the next four hundred years. During that time, Persia fell to Greece, then Greece fell to Rome. Rome was ruling that part of the world when Jesus was born, and the New Testament began.

That sums up the Old Testament. I have left out a few details, but in its skeletal form, that is the historical overview. Not so difficult, eh?

The time span is helpful to understand, also. The first eleven chapters of Genesis record prehistory, and we are not certain how much time passed from Creation to the birth of Abraham. Rounding off the numbers, we find Abraham appearing in Genesis 12 about two thousand years before Christ; Moses, about fifteen hundred years before Christ; David, about a thousand years before Christ; and Ezra about five hundred years before Christ. Some of these figures are "rounder" than others, but they give you the general picture.

Why I Need to Know This

If I don't know this, I will be confused about the story of the Old Testament, uncertain where to find things in the Old Testament, and unsure that the Old Testament really makes sense. Unless I see the overall picture, I will be less able to understand all the little pictures in the Old Testament. It gives me confidence that the Bible really does make sense, and hope that I can gain reasonable mastery over it.

The first seventeen books of the Old Testament, called the historical books, tell the basic story. The next five books, books of poetry, and the last seventeen books, books of prophecy, were all written during the time period covered in the first seventeen books. That makes thirty-nine books, all the books in the Old Testament. If you want to learn the story of the Old Testament, for the most part you have to read only the first seventeen books. Everything else is, in the broad strokes, supplemental to that information.

Old Testament Time Line

Pre-history	2000 B.C.	1500 B.C.	1000 B.C.	500 B.C.	
Adam and Eve	Abraham	Moses	David	Ezra	Jesus

Many people find it astonishing that it is that simple. However, details add color and interest, so for the next part of the chapter, I would like to elaborate on that story and fill in some of the gaps. When fleshing out the skeletal framework of the Old Testament, it can be helpful to break the time span of the Old Testament into eras. I used this common way of handling the material in my book *30 Days to Understanding the Bible*. I will draw gen-

erally on that material as I present the next layer of detail on the
story of the Old Testament.

What Are the Major Eras of Old Testament History?

*The entire story of the Old Testament can be broken into nine major time
periods.*

1. Creation Era (Genesis 1—11)

God created the universe, the world, all that is in the world,
and humankind. Original creation was a paradise, without sin.
Adam and Eve lived in perfect fellowship and harmony with
God, ruling with God over the Garden of Eden. They were individuals of amazing intellect and stunning beauty, created in the
moral, spiritual, and intellectual image of God.

But for reasons that transcend either our
knowledge or our understanding or both, sin
entered the world. Adam and Eve sinned and
were driven out of the Garden of Eden. As
they and their children multiplied, it became
clear that all their descendants inherited their
sinful nature. When Adam and Eve fell, the
whole human race toppled like dominoes
through all the succeeding generations.

Humanity became increasingly wicked as the population bal-
looned, until several hundred years later, by the time of Noah, apparently millions of people dwelt on the earth. God destroyed the
earth with a universal flood as a judgment for the sin of humanity, preserving a righteous remnant in Noah and his immediate
family.

After the flood, God instructed Noah and his family to spread
out and inhabit the whole earth. In direct disobedience to that
command, everyone stayed in one place and began building a
monument to themselves, called the Tower of Babel. As judgment
for this sin and to fulfill the divine mandate to inhabit the whole
earth, God caused the people working on the tower to begin
speaking different languages. Because they could no longer
understand each other, they broke into language groups, and
spread out to form the basis of the nations of the world as we
know them today.

2. Patriarch Era (Genesis 12—50)

"Patriarch" means "great father," and the book of Genesis presents four men who are the patriarchs of Israel. They are Abraham, his son Isaac, Isaac's son Jacob, and Jacob's son Joseph. Genesis first describes four great events: Creation, the Fall, the Flood, and the Tower of Babel. Then it talks about four great men: Abraham, Isaac, Jacob, and Joseph. We will look at each one of them.

God decided to establish a nation that He would bless, and through which He would bless the whole world. He chose Abraham to be the father of this nation, which became Israel. Abraham was living in the city of Ur, near where the Tigris and Euphrates flow into the Persian Gulf, in what would be modern Iraq. God led him to the land of Canaan, which is the land of modern-day Israel, near the present city of Jerusalem. God made a unilateral covenant with Abraham and promised to give him land, descendants and divine blessing. Once in Canaan, Abraham had two sons, Ishmael, from a servant girl, and Isaac, from Abraham's wife, Sarah.

Isaac was the child of the covenant, meaning that the promises given to Abraham for land, descendants, and divine blessing were passed down to Isaac. Isaac lived in the land of Abraham, enjoying prosperity and a long life. He had two sons, Esau and Jacob. Jacob, as son of the covenant, inherited the promises given to Abraham and Isaac. Jacob, at first, was a dishonest, manipulative man, flimflamming and devious the early years of his life. God finally caught his attention, however, and he developed more purpose to his life. Jacob had twelve sons, and this time, instead of one son's being singled out to be the son of the covenant, the promises of Abraham, Isaac, and Jacob passed down to all twelve sons who fathered the twelve tribes or clans in Israel. Every Hebrew person could trace his or her ancestry back to one of these twelve sons.

Jacob's next-to-the-youngest of the twelve sons, Joseph, is, nevertheless, the next main figure on whom the book of Genesis focuses. His being Jacob's favorite son caused resentment among his brothers. So they sold him as a slave to a caravan which took him to Egypt. While there, through a series of acts of God, Joseph rose in power to become second-in-command of the

entire nation of Egypt, and was used by God to save his family in
Canaan from starvation when a severe famine hit. Jacob and all
his sons and grandsons moved to Egypt where they lived for the
next four hundred years.

3. Exodus Era (Exodus—Deuteronomy)

Soon after Joseph died, the Egyptians, viewing the Hebrew
people as a possible military threat because they increased in
numbers so rapidly, enslaved them. Their life as slaves was a very
difficult one, and finally God chose Moses to lead them out of
Egypt, out of slavery, and back into the land which God had
promised to Abraham and his descendants, the modern land of
Israel. The Pharaoh, Egypt's ruler, refused the Israelites' request
to leave in order to have freedom to worship God, so God levied
on the nation of Egypt a series of ten plagues. These terrible
plagues culminated in the death of every first-born child and animal in Egypt except those belonging to the Hebrew people. This
finally convinced Pharaoh to let the Hebrew people go.

They had journeyed as far as the Red Sea
when Pharaoh changed his mind and chased
after them. God parted the Red Sea, the children of Israel crossed over, and the Red Sea
flowed together again, saving them from the
Egyptian army. They then marched to the
southern tip of the Sinai peninsula and
camped at the base of Mt. Sinai, where God
gave Moses the Ten Commandments. God's
intention was to lead them then into the
promised land. But when spies sent to scout Canaan reported giants living in the land, the people rebelled and refused to enter
the land, even though God had promised them victory. As a result, they wandered in the wilderness for forty years until that rebellious generation died. Then, God led the new generation into
the land.

4. Conquest Era (Joshua)

After Moses led the Israelites out of Egypt, shepherded them
for forty years in the wilderness, and brought them to the top of
the Dead Sea, the eastern gateway into the Promised Land
(Canaan), he died. His protégé, Joshua, took over leadership of
the nation. He led them into the Promised Land, and through bril-

liant military leadership, conquered all the fortified cities inside the land which had been promised by God to the Israelites through Abraham. It might seem unfair for the Israelites to displace the people living in that area, but God used Israel as a sword of divine judgment on the Canaanites and other people living there, a people dreadfully degenerate, cruel, evil, and pagan.

5. Judges Era (Judges)

After the conquest of the Promised Land was complete, the people of Israel settled down for the next four hundred years to a relatively normal life as farmers, shepherds, and merchants. Their loose governmental system went into effect basically only if they were threatened militarily by other people. In general, after the land was conquered the people got spiritually lazy and began violating God's law which had been given to them by Moses. In divine judgment for their sin, God would raise up a nation to come in and militarily suppress them. This would cause the Israelites to cry out to God for deliverance. God would give them a deliverer, who was called a "judge." A political, military and religious person, the judge was blessed by God with extraordinary leadership abilities. This judge would lead the nation in a revival which would move God to bless their military efforts, and they would throw off the bonds of their oppressors. This happened

seven times during the four hundred years of the judges. God established the pattern that if Israel would live in a righteous relationship with Him, He would protect them. If they didn't, God would allow them to become vulnerable to other nations. As their leaders went, so went the nation.

6. Kingdom Era (1 Samuel—2 Chronicles)

Finally, the Israelites appealed to God for a king, and God gave them their first king, Saul, of the tribe of Benjamin. Saul led Israel in righteousness for only a short time. So he was removed by God as king (he was killed in battle), and David was made king instead. David led the nation in righteousness all his life, and the nation prospered as at no other time in its history. David died in peace and prosperity at an old age, and his son, Solomon, became king in his place. Solomon led the nation in righteousness for the first part of his forty-year reign, but then fell into sin.

As a result, when Solomon died, God judged the sin of Israel by allowing the nation to divide into a northern kingdom and a southern kingdom. The northern kingdom kept the name "Israel" since ten of the tribes of Israel remained faithful to it. Ruled by a series of nineteen kings, none of which were righteous, Israel lasted for about two hundred fifty years. As a final act of judgment on the nation for its sin, God allowed Assyria, a powerful neighbor to the northeast, to destroy Israel, and it was never restored again.

The southern kingdom adopted the name Judah, because Judah was the largest of the two tribes which were faithful to the southern kingdom. (Benjamin was the other tribe.) They lasted for about one hundred fifty years after the destruction of the northern kingdom. Of their twenty kings, eight were righteous, which explains why the southern kingdom survived longer than the northern kingdom. Righteousness prolonged the life of the nation. Sin shortened it. However, after four hundred years of existence, the southern kingdom was conquered by a powerful neighbor to the east, Babylonia.

7. The Exile Era (Ezekiel—Daniel)

Babylonia had conquered Assyria to the north and was the most powerful country in the area at the time. Babylonia took many of the Hebrew people into captivity to Babylonia for seventy years.

8. The Return Era (Ezra—Esther)

At the end of this seventy-year period, which was prophesied by the prophet Jeremiah, God raised up Persia, to the south of Babylonia, to conquer Babylonia. The king of Persia saw all the Jewish people living in Babylonia and gave them permission to return to Canaan, to rebuild the city of Jerusalem and the temple, and to reinstitute temple worship of God. Fifty thousand people returned from Babylonia to Jerusalem under the leadership of three men: Zerubbabel, Ezra, and Nehemiah. Though Israel was never independent again, it did have reasonable autonomy as far as temple worship was concerned.

9. Silence Era (No books of the Bible written during this time)

Four hundred years passed, during which Persia declined as the dominant military power of the day, and Greece emerged. Then Greece declined as the dominant military power of the day, and Rome emerged. Rome was ruling that part of the world when Jesus was born, and the New Testament era began.

What Was the Geographical Movement of the Old Testament?

The geographical focus of the Israelites moved from Ur (where Abraham first lived), to Canaan (patriarchs), to Egypt (slavery), back to Canaan (which became Israel under the monarchy), to Babylonia (captivity), and back to Jerusalem (return).

We now look at these movements and key locations for each of the nine eras.

1. Creation Era

Creation took place everywhere, of course. The Fall took place in the Garden of Eden. We can't locate the Garden exactly, but we do know it was near where four rivers merged, two of which still exist today, the Tigris and the Euphrates. This probably puts the Garden of Eden somewhere in the ancient region of Babylonia and in the modern country of Iraq. Nothing in Iraq today resembles even the shadow of the Garden of Eden, but that is because of the effects of the Fall. When sin entered the world, it damaged not only mankind, but the earth as well. What was once a paradise is now a desert. (See map at top of page 74.)

Most of the activity described in the Old Testament took place in this area, known as the ancient Near East.

Draw an arrow from Ur, where Abraham lived, to Canaan, and from Canaan to Egypt, to represent the geographical movements of the Patriarch Era.

2. Patriarch Era

God first revealed himself to Abraham when Abraham was living in the city of Ur, just north of the modern Persian Gulf. Abraham migrated west to where modern Jerusalem is. He lived in that general area the rest of his life. So did his son Isaac, and Isaac's son, Jacob. Jacob's son, Joseph, was sold into slavery in Egypt and all Jacob's family eventually joined him there. (See map at the bottom of page 74.)

3. Exodus Era

Moses led the Israelites out of Egypt, across the Red Sea, south to the bottom of the Sinai peninsula, then north to the oasis of Kadesh Barnea. There the nation rebelled, and wandered in the wilderness of Sinai and south and east of the Dead Sea for forty years. Then Moses led them near to where the Jordan River flows into the Dead Sea, and there he died. (East of Kadesh Barnea are three connected bodies of water. Moving north they are the Dead Sea, the Jordan River, and the Sea of Galilee.)

Draw an arrow from Egypt through the Red Sea to Mount Sinai to Kadesh Barnea, and then to the top of the Dead Sea on the east side of the Jordan River. This represents the geographical movement of the Exodus Era.

4. The Conquest Era

Joshua led the Israelites into the Promised Land at Jericho and marched westward to the western city of Ai. This cut the land of Canaan in half. They conquered the southern part of Canaan first, before sweeping into the northern part of Canaan.

Draw an arrow from Jericho across to the Mediterranean Sea. Then draw an arrow into the southern half of the land. Now draw an arrow into the northern half of the land. This represents the geographical movement of the Conquest Era.

5. The Judges Era

There is no geographical movement during the Judges Era. The Israelites were consumed with trying to establish themselves in the Promised Land, even while being plagued by occasional military encroachment by their neighbors.

6. The Kingdom Era

When Assyria conquered the northern kingdom of Israel, the land area generally west of the Sea of Galilee and Jordan River was lost, and the people were scattered. When Babylonia conquered the southern kingdom, the land area generally west of the Dead Sea was lost and the leaders were taken into captivity in Babylonia. (See map on page 77.)

7. Exile Era

The exile took the Israelites into Babylon, which was located northeast of Jerusalem, on the Euphrates River, in modern-day Iraq.

Draw an arrow from Israel to Assyria. Draw another arrow from Judah to Babylonia. This represents the geographical movement of the Kingdom Era.

There is no geographical movement during the Exile Era since the captive Israelites remained in Babylonia for seventy years. However, near the end of that time Babylonia was conquered and ruled by Persia.

8. The Return Era

By decree of their new Persian ruler, the return brought 50,000 Jews back from captivity in Babylonia to Jerusalem, to rebuild the city, the walls and the temple. (See map on page 78.)

Draw an arrow from Persia to Jerusalem to represent geographical movements during the Return Era.

Conclusion

The entire story of the Old Testament took place in a geographical setting no larger than the state of Texas. The Promised Land, corresponding roughly to the modern nation of Israel, is only about one hundred thirty miles long and fifty miles wide. When broken down into its parts, with the story stripped of all but the essentials, the history and geography of the Old Testament are fairly simple and easily grasped.

Speed Bump!

Question Answer

Q1. What is the capsule summary of the Old Testament?

A1. The Old Testament is primarily the story of God's dealings with humanity through the nation of *Israel*.

Q2. What are the major eras of Old Testament history?

A2. The entire story of the Old Testament can be broken into *nine* major time periods.

Q3. What was the geographical movement of the Old Testament?

A3. The geographical focus of the Israelites *moved* from Ur (where Abraham first lived), to Canaan (patriarchs), to Egypt (slavery), back to Canaan (which became Israel under the monarchy), to Babylonia (captivity), and back to Jerusalem (return).

Fill in the Blank

Question Answer

Q1. What is the capsule summary of the Old Testament?

A1. The Old Testament is primarily the story of God's dealings with humanity through the nation of

_____.

Q2. What are the major eras of Old Testament history?

A2. The entire story of the Old Testament can be broken into _____ major time periods.

Q3. What was the geographical movement of the Old Testament?

A3. The geographical focus of the Israelites _____ from Ur (where Abraham first lived), to Canaan (patriarchs), to Egypt (slavery), back to Canaan (which became Israel under the monarchy), to Babylonia (captivity), and back to Jerusalem (return).

For Further Thought and Discussion

1. Compare a modern map of Texas with a Bible map showing the geographic movement of the events of the Old Testament. It will help you gain a much better feel for the story of the Old Testament.

2. What town is about one hundred thirty miles from you? On a map of your state (in pencil, if you wish), draw a box fifty miles wide from your town to the town one hundred thirty miles from you. This is the general land area of the land of Israel.

3. In what way does an understanding of the story and geography of the Old Testament most help you?

What If I Don't Believe?

This material does not deal with any interpretation of spiritual information, but merely presents facts. If I believe that the Bible is historically and geographically accurate, I can take this information at face value, even if I don't take the spiritual message of the Bible at face value. If I don't believe that the Bible is historically and geographically accurate, then the Bible is little more than a book of mythology or fanciful tales.

For Further Study

30 Days to Understanding the Bible, Max Anders

Note: The era drawings and maps are taken from this book and used by permission of the publisher, Word, Inc. The material in this chapter is expanded considerably in *30 Days to Understanding the Bible*, and you are encouraged to read it when you have completed this book.

What the Bible Is All About, Henrietta Mears
Talk thru the Bible, Ken Boa and Bruce Wilkinson

The New Testament is the very best book that ever was or ever will be known in the world.
■ Charles Dickens

6

What Is the Story of the New Testament?

On a plaque marking Abraham Lincoln's birthplace near Hodgenville, Kentucky, is recorded this scrap of conversation:

"Any news down t' the village, Ezry?"

"Well, Squire McLain's gone t' Washington t' see Madison swore in, and al' Spellman tells me this Bonapart fella has captured most of Spain. What's new out here, neighbor?"

"Nuthin', nuthin' a'tall, 'cept fer a new baby born t' Tom Lincoln's. Nuthin' ever happens out here."

We smile at the conversation, because on that day, the birth of a baby didn't seem very important compared to a new president in Washington and a conquering emperor in Europe. But in the end, Abraham Lincoln grew to be more important than either. What seems important and unimportant to us often gets mixed up.

So it is with the Bible. If you were to ask the average person on the street today what is important, he would likely mention something in news, weather, or sports. But the truth of the Bible, in the end, will prove out to be much more important than anything else we might hear of the day's news, weather or sports.

Beginning a mastery of the New Testament is one of the greatest quests we can undertake, and a good beginning point is to grasp the major people, places and events. The New Testament is much less complex than the Old; the story simpler, the time span shorter, and the geographical movement less. Yet it is just as helpful to understand the story of the New Testament as it is the Old. Like the Old, it is simpler than many people realize, and the satisfaction of knowing the story and how all the books fit together can motivate us to become better Bible students.

What Is the Capsule Summary of the New Testament?

The New Testament is primarily the story of Jesus' dealings with humanity through the church.

The skeletal story line of the New Testament is fairly simple. Jesus was born in Bethlehem near Jerusalem, according to Old Testament prophecy. Then Jesus and His parents, Mary and Joseph, moved back to their hometown in Nazareth in the northern part of the country, just east of the Sea of Galilee. There, with few details from Scripture, Jesus lived an apparently normal childhood and adulthood until He turned thirty. At the age of thirty, the age at which all teachers by Jewish custom began their ministry, Jesus left Nazareth and went to Jerusalem. He began His initial ministry there and the surrounding area of Judea.

Shortly after, He went north to the area around the Sea of Galilee, making Capernaum His home base. Capernaum was located on the north shore of the Sea of Galilee. He conducted much of His three-year ministry while home-based at Capernaum, although many events did not actually take place in Capernaum, but in the surrounding area. Eventually, He returned to Jerusalem and was crucified. Three days later, He rose from the dead and showed Himself to His disciples several times over the next forty days. Then, with His disciples gathered around Him on the Mount of Olives, just east of Jerusalem, He visibly ascended into heaven.

He had commissioned His disciples to take the new message of salvation through Christ to Jerusalem, Judea, and Samaria (the surrounding regions), and to the uttermost parts of the earth. The fulfillment of this command focuses primarily on the apostle Paul who made three missionary journeys to surrounding areas in Asia Minor and Greece. Finally, Paul was arrested and taken to Rome, where he eventually died. Enough disciples remained, however, in Jerusalem, Asia Minor, Greece, and Rome, that the message not only lived on, but mushroomed into a major world religion.

What Are the Major Eras of New Testament History?

The entire story of the New Testament can be broken into three major time periods.

1. The Gospels Era (Matthew—John)

Many Jews lived in Jerusalem and the surrounding area west of the Sea of Galilee, the Jordan River, and the Dead Sea. These people descended from those who had been left there when the Babylonians conquered the southern kingdom, and those who returned from captivity seventy years later.

Several different groups of people lived there, with the city of Jerusalem and the temple being the focal point of their lives. First were the Pharisees, conservative religious leaders of Israel who stringently separated themselves from the Gentiles who surrounded them. They had many traditions which they had elevated in importance to the level of Scripture itself. Jesus even accused them of violating Scripture in order to keep their own traditions.

A second group, the Sadducees, led the liberal religious camp. They were more conciliatory toward interaction with Gentiles and less scrupulous about keeping traditions. These "big money" people had decided to get along with everyone in order to prosper personally.

Third were zealots, political fanatics who willingly risked their very lives to overthrow the Romans and set up Israel as a sovereign nation again.

Finally, there were the ordinary citizens, neither Pharisees nor Sadducees nor political fanatics, but common folk trying to put bread on the table, clothing on their backs, and a roof over their heads; people who went to their synagogues and to the Temple, and worshiped God the best way they knew how.

All these groups had one thing in common—a deep longing for the coming of the Messiah, the Promised One of the Old Testament who would come and free Israel and set everything right. Each group had a different concept of who the Messiah would be and how He would go about bringing them deliverance, but all of them lived with a heightened messianic expectation.

Whatever their concept of the Messiah, Jesus did not fit it. No one expected a stable-born man from an obscure village, unknown and unrecognized until His thirtieth birthday. In His lifetime, opinion about Him was as widely divided as it is now. Yet the birth of Jesus towers as the great continental divide of history. He is the Mount Everest of history. Everything before Him flows B.C., before Christ; everything after Him flows A.D., *anno Domini*, the year of our Lord. The calendar was changed because of Him; governments changed because of Him; the course of history changed because of Him. And all this, because multiplied millions of people have been transformed because of Him.

The first four books of the New Testament—Matthew, Mark, Luke, John—tell His story. However, while biographical, they are not intended to be complete pictures of His life. They all spend a great deal of time on His birth and death, and almost no time on His first thirty years. Matthew, Mark, and Luke cover much of the same material, underscoring the humanity of Jesus; John's perspective emphasizes His deity. All four Gospels, when superimposed on each other, present only about fifty days of Jesus' active ministry.

In this chapter we learn that . . .

1. The New Testament is primarily the story of Jesus' dealings with humanity through the church.
2. The entire story of the New Testament can be broken into three major time periods.
3. The geographical focus of the New Testament moved from Bethlehem to Jerusalem to Capernaum and back to Jerusalem; then to Asia Minor and Greece.

The story, however, goes like this: Jesus' birth to the Virgin Mary resulted from a miraculous conception brought about by the Holy Spirit. Both birth and place of birth—Bethlehem of Judea, a small village near Jerusalem—fulfilled an Old Testament prophecy. Although His parents, Mary and Joseph, lived in Nazareth, they had to travel to Bethlehem when a Roman census required Joseph to be registered in the city of his ancestry. The ruler over that part of the country, Herod, wanted to kill Jesus because Herod saw Him as a threat to his throne, so Mary and Joseph, being warned in a dream by God, fled to Egypt until Herod died. They then returned to Nazareth, and there Jesus learned the trade of a carpenter and lived an apparently uneventful life until he turned thirty, at which age Jewish men could begin a ministry.

Isaiah prophesied in the Old Testament (Isaiah 40:3–5) that a prophet would precede the coming of the Messiah. That prophet was John the Baptist, who happened to be Jesus' cousin. He urged people to "repent, for the kingdom of heaven is at hand" (Matthew 3:2) and preached that one would come after him whose sandals John would not be worthy to carry (Matthew 3:11). John was baptizing people in the Jordan River near the Dead Sea, and Jesus went there to have John baptize Him. Upon His being baptized, the heavens opened and He saw the Spirit of God descending like a dove and alighting upon Him. Then God the Father spoke from heaven, saying, "This is my beloved Son, in whom I am well pleased" (Matthew 3:16–17).

Afterward, the Holy Spirit led Jesus out into the wilderness where Satan tempted Him to depart from God's will for His life. Jesus passed that grueling, difficult trial, remaining sinless and validating His readiness to make Himself known as the Messiah.

Why I Need to Know This

If I don't know this, I will be confused about the story of the New Testament and uncertain where to find things in the New Testament. Knowing what was happening historically and geographically helps me understand some of the New Testament books better. Unless I see the overall picture, I will be less able to understand all the little pictures in the New Testament. The stories of the Old and New Testaments together give me confidence that the Bible really does make sense, and hope that I can gain reasonable mastery over it.

His early ministry began in and around Jerusalem where the public initially accepted Him. His twofold message declared first, that He was the predicted Messiah and that people should believe in Him for salvation; and second, that people should pursue genuine righteousness, not the external hypocrisy so common among the religious leaders. In addition, He performed astonishing miracles which lent credibility to His message and had the people of the entire area talking about Him.

His initial popularity did not last, however, for two reasons. First, when the religious leaders finally understood that Jesus was condemning their practice of empty religion, they felt threatened by the message and jealous of His growing following. Therefore, they tried to find ways of opposing Him. Second, it became apparent that many of the people who followed Him were doing so not because they truly believed the message He was proclaiming, but because His miracles intrigued or benefitted them.

Because of a growing resistance to His message, Jesus began spending more and more time with just His twelve disciples, preparing them to carry on without Him. At the same time, He challenged the multitudes to count the cost of following Him. Though Jesus traveled quite a bit during this time, His home base was Capernaum.

The Jewish people became more and more polarized about Jesus. The warnings to the multitudes to count the cost of following Him caused the people either to follow Him enthusiastically or resent Him deeply. Finally, during the time of a Jewish holiday when many Jews were in Jerusalem, the religious leaders, jealous of His following and threatened by Jesus' growing attacks on their hypocrisy, stirred up the multitude to demand Jesus' crucifixion. They subjected Him to a series of unjust trials on false charges. Pilate, the Roman ruler of Jerusalem, did not want to convict Him, but public sentiment ran so high that to do otherwise might risk a riot. Since that would not look good on Pilate's record as governor, he caved in and ordered Jesus' crucifixion.

Jesus was executed and buried, lay in the tomb for three days, and then rose from the dead. He presented Himself to His disciples to prove to them that He was alive, told them that He would soon be leaving, and commissioned them to spread the gospel of salvation by grace through faith in Jesus to the uttermost parts of the earth.

2. The Church Era (Acts 1—8)

Having completed the preparations for His departure, Jesus ascended into heaven from the Mount of Olives with His followers gathered around Him. He had instructed His disciples to wait in Jerusalem until they were given power from on high, after which they were to witness about Him to the uttermost parts of the earth.

Ten days after Jesus' ascension into heaven, the church was born in Jerusalem. The disciples were assembled together in a house on the Jewish feast day of Pentecost when the Holy Spirit suddenly came upon them. A sound like a violent, rushing wind filled the place, and flames like fire rested on each one of them, and they began speaking in different tongues as they were filled with the Holy Spirit. These tongues were foreign languages, and when this noise occurred, a large crowd from many different countries gathered at the house, and heard the followers of Jesus each speaking in the listener's own language. Many other miracles happened in the early days of the church, and converts to Christianity increased rapidly.

All this multitude of believers had to be organized. Many of the Jews who joined the young church came from other countries. They had left their homes and livelihood to go to Jerusalem for the holiday of Pentecost, and perhaps had run out of money. Some of those who had possessions sold them and brought the money to the apostles to care for those in need. Special people called "deacons" were to look after the physical needs of the early converts while the apostles looked after their spiritual needs.

The animosity that the religious leaders had toward Jesus was now directed toward the increasing number of his followers. They arrested Stephen, who was one of the deacons, for preaching about Jesus. They tried to get him to deny Jesus, but he would not, so they stoned him to death. Thus Stephen became the first known martyr of the church.

3. The Missions Era (Acts 9—28)

One of the most vicious persecutors of the early Christians was a Pharisee named Saul. After creating havoc among the Christians in Jerusalem, he left for Damascus in Syria to find and persecute Christians there. On the way, Jesus appeared to him in a blinding vision, and Saul was converted to Christianity. His name was changed to Paul, and he became the greatest missionary of that time, ministering to the Gentiles. In three missionary journeys to Asia Minor and Greece, Paul was used by God to lead many Gentiles to Christ and to establish many churches throughout the region.

The first missionary journey, a two-year trip, took him to

Galatia in Asia Minor (modern Turkey). On the second missionary journey, one that lasted three years, he sailed to Macedonia in
modern Greece. And finally, his third missionary trip traversed
Asia, a region in modern Turkey where he ministered for four
years. On all three missionary journeys he left from Antioch, a
town in Asia Minor very near the Syrian border.

Paul then returned to Jerusalem, where he was arrested on
false charges. A Roman citizen, he appealed to Rome to plead his
case before Caesar. The Bible does not give us the final details, but
we think that Paul died in Rome, having been executed for the
false charges.

Most of the rest of the books of the New Testament were written by Paul, Peter, or John during the time period covered in the
book of Acts, but some after the close of the book of Acts. However, while providing much-needed instructions for the Christian
life, they generally don't provide much more of the story of the
church.

What Was the Geographical Movement of the New Testament?

*The geographical focus of the New Testament moved from Bethlehem
to Jerusalem to Capernaum and back to Jerusalem; then to Asia Minor
and Greece.*

Let us now look at these movements and key locations for
each era.

1. The Gospels Era

The geographical movement in the Gospels Era followed Jesus' life. Born in Bethlehem, He fled shortly after that with His
parents to Egypt. When it was safe to come back into Palestine after the death of Herod, who tried to kill Him, they went back
home to Nazareth. Jesus lived there until He began His ministry.
He centered His early ministry around Jerusalem. Then, He
moved north to Capernaum, and home-based there for much
of His ministry. Then, as the final events in His life began to
draw to a climax, His travels took Him to Jerusalem, and He
never left. He died and arose there, and ascended to heaven from
that area. (See map on page 89.)

Draw an arrow from Bethlehem to Egypt to Nazareth to represent the geographical movement in Jesus' early life, and label it 1. Draw an arrow from Nazareth to Jerusalem to represent His initial acceptance, and label it 2. Draw an arrow from Jerusalem to Capernaum to represent the growing rejection, and label it 3. Draw an arrow from Capernaum to Jerusalem to represent His final rejection, and label it 4.

2. The Church Era

There is no geographical movement during the Church Era, since the church remained close to Jerusalem until persecution began, which ushered in the Missions Era.

3. The Missions Era

The geographical movement in the Missions Era followed the missionary journeys of Paul. His first missionary journey took him to Galatia in modern Turkey. He returned to Jerusalem for a time before setting out on his second missionary journey. This took him back to Galatia and on to Macedonia in modern Greece, after which he returned to Jerusalem.

His final missionary journey took him to Asia near the Aegean Sea in modern Turkey, and back to Jerusalem. Then, he went to Rome to defend himself against false charges, where he died. (See map on page 90.)

Draw an arrow from Antioch to Galatia and put a 1 next to it. Draw an arrow from Antioch to Greece and put a 2 next to it. Draw an arrow from Antioch to Asia and put a 3 next to it. This represents the geographical movement of Paul's missionary journeys. Now, draw an arrow from Caesarea to Rome and put a 4 next to it to represent Paul's trials and imprisonment during the Missions Era.

Conclusion

The entire story of the Gospels took place in a geographical setting not much larger than the very small state of Connecticut. Jesus' travels for the most part did not exceed the distance from Jerusalem to Capernaum, about eighty miles north to south, and from the Sea of Galilee to Nazareth, about ten or fifteen miles east to west.

The apostle Paul traveled nearly fifteen hundred miles on his third missionary journey, and nearly two thousand miles on his trip to Rome.

The story of the New Testament, like the Old, when stripped to its essentials, is fairly simple.

Speed Bump!

Q**uestion**
A**nswer**

Q1. What is the capsule summary of the New Testament?

A1. The New Testament is primarily the story of Jesus' dealings with humanity through the *church*.

Q2. What are the major eras of New Testament history?

A2. The entire story of the New Testament can be broken into *three* major time periods.

Q3. What was the geographical movement of the New Testament?

A3. The geographical focus of the New Testament *moved* from Bethlehem to Jerusalem to Capernaum and back to Jerusalem; then to Asia Minor and Greece.

Fill in the Blank

Q**uestion**
A**nswer**

Q1. What is the capsule summary of the New Testament?

A1. The New Testament is primarily the story of Jesus' dealings with humanity through the _____.

Q2. What are the major eras of New Testament history?

A2. The entire story of the New Testament can be broken into _____ major time periods.

Q3. What was the geographical movement of the New Testament?

A3. The geographical focus of the New Testament _____ from Bethlehem to Jerusalem to Capernaum and back to Jerusalem; then to Asia Minor and Greece.

For Further Thought and Discussion

1. Compare a modern map of your state with the map showing the geographic movement of the events of the New Testament. It will help you gain a much better feel for the story of the New Testament.

2. What town is about eighty miles from you? On a map of your state, (in pencil, if you wish) draw a box twenty-five miles wide from your town

to the town eighty miles from you. Except for His trip into Egypt as a child, this is the general land area in which Jesus traveled.

3. In what way does an understanding of the story and geography of the New Testament most help you?

What If I Don't Believe?

Just as in the Old Testament, there is little here not to believe, since this chapter does not deal with any interpretation of spiritual information, but merely presents the main people, places, and events of the New Testament. If I believe that the New Testament is historically and geographically accurate, I can take this information at face value, even if I don't take the spiritual message of the New Testament the same way. If I don't believe in the historical and geographical accuracy of the New Testament, then the Bible becomes only a book of mythology or historical fiction.

For Further Study

30 Days to Understanding the Bible, Max Anders.
Note: The era drawings and maps are taken from this book and used by permission of the publisher, Word, Inc. The material in this chapter is expanded considerably in *30 Days to Understanding the Bible*, and you are encouraged to read it when you have completed this book.

What the Bible Is All About, Henrietta Mears
Talk thru the Bible, Ken Boa and Bruce Wilkinson

*I want to know one thing—the way to
heaven; how to land safe on that happy shore.
God Himself has condescended to teach the
way: For this very end He came from heaven.
He hath written it down in a book. O give me
that book! At any price, give me the book of
God! I have it: Here is knowledge enough for
me. Let me be a man of one book.*
■ John Wesley

7

What Is the Message
of the Bible?

The skeletal story line of the Civil War includes the battles of Gettysburg, Vicksburg, Chattanooga, Atlanta, and Richmond. It relates the deeds of Grant, Lee, Sherman, and Lincoln. It concerns slavery, self-rule, and economic independence. But the *message* of the Civil War is that the preservation of the Union was worth risking one's life.

The basic story line of the civil rights movement includes Martin Luther King, Jr., nonviolent protests by blacks, violent retaliations by whites, court orders, and civil rights laws. But the message of the civil rights movement declares that all people, black and white, are created equal in the eyes of God, and therefore should be treated equally under the law and by one another.

We find this same parallel in the Bible. The message of the Bible differs from the basic story line of the Bible. The story line involves the major people, places, and events of the Bible in their proper chronological order. But the message of the Bible is what God was doing in and through people as the story progressed. The message is the truth that permeates the historical events. So after looking at the story line of the Bible, it is only logical that we should examine the message of the Bible.

The message of the Bible answers the question "Why has God spoken?" His self-sufficiency does not need our gifts or service (Acts 17:25). Why, then, does He bother to speak to us? James I. Packer answers that question in his book, *God Has Spoken:*

> The truly staggering answer which the Bible gives to this question is that God's purpose in revelation is to *make friends* with us. It was to this end that He created us rational beings, bearing His image, able to think and hear and speak and love; He wanted there to be genuine personal affection and friendship, two-sided, between Himself and us—a relation, not like that between a man and his dog, but like that of a father to his son, or a husband to his wife. Loving friendship between two persons has no ulterior motive; it is an end in itself. And that is God's end in revelation. He speaks to us simply to fulfill the purpose for which we were made; that is, to bring into being a relationship in which He is a friend to us, and we to Him, He finding His joy in giving us gifts and we finding ours in giving Him thanks (50).

In this chapter we learn that . . .

1. The message of the Bible is that God is demonstrating to the universe through us that He is who He says He is.
2. The Old Testament focuses on the temporary solution God provided to humanity's sin problem.
3. The New Testament focuses on the permanent solution God has provided in Christ to humanity's sin problem.

That explains why He has spoken. In the remainder of the chapter, we will look more closely at what is involved in our receiving such a gracious relationship with God.

What Is the Message of the Bible?

The message of the Bible is that God is demonstrating to the universe through us that He is who He says He is.

God says that He is all-knowing, all-powerful, everywhere present simultaneously; that He is loving, merciful, and just. Many people would say that the evidence around us proves just the opposite—that either He does not care about the suffering of humanity or that He cannot do anything about it. Someone once said that the fact that celery is good for you, but hot fudge is bad for you proves there is no God. We are supposed to smile at such a comment, but there is a deep and subtle truth behind it.

God wants to prove that in spite of apparent evidence to the contrary, He is perfect in His character and able to perform whatever He chooses. In spite of the pain, suffering, and injustice we see in the world, God is who He says He is.

In demonstrating to the universe through us that God is who He says He is, His goal is to bring glory to Himself and pleasure to us. The Westminster Confession, a seventeenth-century statement of faith still used in many churches today, states that the chief end of man is to glorify God and enjoy Him forever. This startling statement negates the concept of God as a cosmic killjoy, and brings up several questions. First, who does God say He is? Second, how does He demonstrate through us that He is who He says He is? Third, why does God want to be glorified; and fourth, how does man enjoy Him forever?

1. Who Does God Say He Is?

Another volume in this series, *God: Knowing Our Creator*, treats this topic more fully. Nevertheless, we can summarize the answer here. God says He is the eternal supreme being, the creator of the universe. He is holy, loving, just, merciful, unchanging, all-knowing, all-powerful, and present everywhere simultaneously.

Holy defines God as without sin, without corruption, without contamination of anything that is not good. For God to be *loving* means that He desires nothing but good for another. For Him to be *just* means, in part, that He applies penalties for sin equally to everyone without partiality. It also means that if a penalty is paid, punishment is rescinded. God as *merciful* means that He offers a way of escape to those who deserve judgment. As He expresses these moral characteristics, He does so without ever changing and with full knowledge, power, and presence to do whatever He wills.

2. How Does He Demonstrate through Us that He Is Who He Says He Is?

God created the universe to be a paradise in which He would live in fellowship with humanity. However, sin contaminated humanity and all other creation. The Bible does not tell us how or why this defilement first happened. The sin of Adam and Eve goes back to the temptation of Satan, but two questions persist: Why did Adam and Eve sin if they were living in paradise in fellowship with God? And where did sin come from in the first place? We don't know the answer to those questions. We know sin originated with Satan, a once-righteous angel who served God. But the Bible simply says that one day sin was found in him (Ezekiel 28:15). It doesn't say where the sin came from, or why God ever allowed it, or why God didn't destroy Satan before he had a chance to contaminate humanity. Scholars have debated these questions for centuries. While we can offer educated and wise speculation, we cannot say for sure because the Bible does not tell us.

God has revealed Himself to us simply to make friends with us.

How does He demonstrate through us that He is who He says He is? To answer that question, we must simply start from where we are. Sin exists. It entered the world through Adam and Eve when they were living in the Garden of Eden. As a result, everyone who would ever be born would be contaminated by sin. That contamination ends in spiritual death—eternal separation from God. Why? Because a holy God cannot abide the presence of sin, and because He is just, He applies the penalty of sin equally to all. However, because God is also merciful and loving, He did not want to leave humanity in its sin. Therefore, He sent His own Son to die for us. Since Jesus became a man, He could die. Because He was God, He never sinned, and His righteousness could extend to others. His one life could save all lives from eternal separation from God. His righteousness, knowledge, power, and presence were enough to satisfy the penalty for sin. For everyone. For all time.

Therefore, by God's plan to redeem from sin and restore humanity to a righteous relationship to Himself through Jesus, God is demonstrating to the universe through us that He is who He says He is. This demonstration not only benefits humanity, but it also manifests to the heavenly powers that He is who He says He is (Colossians 2:13–15).

3. Why Does God Want to Be Glorified?

We don't know all the reasons why God wants to bring glory to Himself. God certainly deserves glory because of the perfection of His being. But does that qualify Him as a cosmic egomaniac? That is what some cynics claim. How do we avoid the perception?

For God to glorify Himself simply means to call accurate attention to who He is. When we glorify God, we simply tell the truth about God. When we live in a way that glorifies God, we are living demonstrations and living mouthpieces of the truth about God. God is the greatest of all beings, perfect in character and capable of doing whatever He wishes. He wishes to do good for us. It is that simple. That is one reason He desires to bring glory to Himself.

> **To glorify God means simply to tell the truth about Him.**

What is the alternative for God or for us? Should God lie about Himself? Should we lie about God? It is not the result of an inflated ego for God to desire to be glorified. Rather, it is His desire for us to know the truth about Him, so that we can avoid the Great Negative—misery in this life and then dying and going to hell—and experience the Great Positive—joy in this life and then dying and going to heaven.

Humanity benefits when God is glorified, because then we know the truth. Where that truth is acknowledged, proclaimed, and cherished, life becomes increasingly like the life God intended us to experience when He created us. It becomes increasingly like the life He wants us to experience forever in heaven. It allows us to become increasingly like God.

The reverse happens also: For humanity not to glorify God is to accept the most fundamental deception, to suppress the most fundamental truth, and so to drift into the fog of confusion and evil, for evil thrives in falsehood, error, and untruth.

Not to glorify God is to poison life so that it becomes increasingly like hell. Everything about God is good, and everything that is not true of God is bad. The closer a person is to being like God, the better off he is; and the less like God a person is, the worse off he is. So we don't have to visualize God as some cosmic egomaniac, demanding adulation at the expense of others. Rather, His glory results in just the opposite.

> **Not to glorify God is to promote deception and to poison life so it becomes like hell.**

We see a great example of this in Isaiah 6:1–8. God reveals himself in great glory:

In the year that King Uzziah died, I saw the Lord sitting on a throne, high and lifted up, and the train of His robe filled the temple. Above it stood seraphim; each one had six wings; with two he covered his face, with two he covered his feet, and with two he flew. And one cried to another and said:

"Holy, holy, holy is the LORD of hosts;
The whole earth is full of His glory!"

And the posts of the door were shaken by the voice of him who cried out, and the house was filled with smoke. (vv. 1–4)

Based on the glory of God which Isaiah witnessed, he knew that God was holy and he was unholy. His unholiness cut him off from God. He was terrified, and he repented deeply:

So I said:
"Woe is me, for I am undone!
Because I am a man of unclean lips,
And I dwell in the midst of a people of unclean lips;
For my eyes have seen the King,
The Lord of hosts." (v. 5)

Because Isaiah repented, his sins were forgiven, and he was cleansed and restored to fellowship with God:

Then one of the seraphim flew to me, having in his hand a live coal which he had taken with tongs from the altar. And he touched my mouth with it, and said:

"Behold, this has touched your lips;
Your iniquity is taken away,
And your sin purged" (vv. 6–7).

God's glory illuminates truth that moves us to repentance and the pleasure of fellowship with Him.

Because Isaiah repented and was restored to fellowship with God, he could now be used by God on a scale that was not possible before:

Also I heard the voice of the Lord, saying:
"Whom shall I send,
And who will go for Us?"
Then I said, "Here am I! Send me" (v. 8).

God revealed His glory to Isaiah. That glory caused Isaiah to see the truth: God was holy and he was unholy. He repented of his unholiness, was forgiven, restored to fellowship with God, and used greatly by Him. Perceiving God's glory gives us an opportunity to repent, which demonstrates the goodness of God, for

He is "not willing that any should perish but that all should come to repentance" (2 Peter 3:9).

I don't mean that we come to God simply for reasons of personal comfort. It is much deeper than that. But as far as God's motivation is concerned, this understanding destroys the misconception that He is a heartless cosmic egomaniac, requiring obeisance from humanity even though that obeisance is hurtful to them. That is like some volcano god who requires the sacrifice of a virgin to him every spring or else he will spew molten lava all over the village. That misconception we want to avoid. God is not so small.

On the other hand, the desire to avoid pain and to pursue pleasure is not to be ignored. God tells us about hell, its misery and torment, and implores us to accept Him so that we don't have to go there. He also tells us about the glories and pleasures of heaven, so that we will *want* to go there. To want pain and to avoid pleasure is unnatural. God has created us for pleasure and not for pain. Pain signals that something is wrong. That is why He has done everything in His power, short of destroying our wills, to get us to receive Him. He wants us to live with Him forever in heaven.

A second misconception I want to avoid is the notion that all pain we experience in this life comes about because we have failed God somehow. If that were the case, Jesus' pain on the cross would be a result of His failure, and that is impossible, because Jesus was without sin or **Much pain we experience comes simply from our existence in a fallen world.** shortcoming of any kind. No, Christians suffer in this world because it is a fallen world, and until all sin and evil is destroyed, we will become casualties to it. Christians will still get diseases, just as non-Christians do. We will still have accidents, and be maltreated, just as non-Christians are. Many of us experience unavoidable pain simply because we live in a fallen world.

Beyond the unavoidable pain, however, we can prevent much pain that *is* avoidable by living in close fellowship and trusting obedience to God. Sin triggers a powerful law of cause and effect. The apostle Paul wrote in Galatians 6:7–8, "Do not be deceived, God is not mocked; for whatever a man sows, that he will also reap. For he who sows to his flesh will of the flesh reap corruption, but he who sows to the Spirit will of the Spirit reap everlasting life."

If you sow anger, you reap anger. If you sow sexual immorality, you reap physical and psychological damage, if you sow selfishness, you reap loneliness, and so on. The closer one lives to God, the more he will reap the fruit of the Spirit: love, joy, peace, patience, kindness, goodness, faithfulness, gentleness, self-control (Galatians 5:22–23). In the next world, of course, nothing but pleasure exists for the child of God, and nothing but pain persists for the one who rejects God. All humankind will either reap pleasure in heaven or harvest pain in hell.

Why I Need to Know This

I need to know this so that I realize that understanding the Bible is more than just becoming acquainted with the people, places, and events of the Bible. A greater message transcends the story, and that greater message is what must ultimately find a home in my heart.

So God is not being selfish when He wants to bring glory to Himself. We may not be able to understand all the reasons why God desires to bring glory to Himself, but the ultimate good of humanity is surely one we can all happily accept.

4. How Do Humans Enjoy God Forever?

We have already answered it, but let's set it in another context to emphasize it. We enjoy God by being like God. Let me give you a true example (the names and circumstances have been changed). Some friends of mine, Bill and Susan, are rural, quiet, uncomplicated, hardworking Christians of uncommon integrity and spiritual depth and insight. Some years ago, they adopted a twelve-year-old Korean-American boy named Lee from San Francisco. His mother was a prostitute and his father unknown. He lived primarily in the streets, was often abused, never had enough to eat, was perpetually dirty, loud, aggressive, and careless. When Lee came to live with Bill and Susan, his circumstances changed radically. From city to country, from no family to a close family, from poverty to plenty, from dirty to clean, from unstructured to structured, from no responsibility to much responsibility, from sloppy to tidy, from no discipline to discipline, from unchristian to Christian—if he had been brought from the back side of the moon, the difference would not have been greater.

Although Lee was glad to be out of San Francisco, his new life in the country disconcerted him. He disliked the structure, discipline, and work, but he appreciated the safety and positively reveled in three meals a day, a warm bed, and clean clothes. Lee immediately modified his behavior. He became reserved, polite, cautious, and friendly. It was his way of playing it safe.

But then, as he relaxed in a safe, loving environment, a transformation took place. As he developed over the next few years into a powerfully built young man, he lost the politeness, caution, and friendliness induced by insecurity. As he shed his insecurity, his real personality reasserted itself. He became quiet, sullen, withdrawn, moody, belligerent, and uncooperative. This personality shift caused confusion and heartache for Bill and Susan. Everything had been going well, and they thought Lee had adapted happily to his new life.

However, they continued to love and accept him while at the same time requiring respectful and responsible speech and behavior. If he complied, things went smoothly; if he didn't, there was always a price to pay, commensurate with the infraction. They were remarkably consistent. "Lee," they would tell him, "we love you as our own son, we will do whatever is in our power to make your life better. We will never stop loving you. But you must understand that we will not accept belligerent behavior, irresponsibility, or immorality. If you break the rules, you must pay the consequences." They exhibited an almost superhuman example of the balance of love and discipline which Dr. James Dobson presents in his book *Dare to Discipline*.

The more God transforms us into His likeness, the more we enjoy Him.

For some time, their discipline did not seem to be working. Lee became particularly rebellious, so Bill and Susan sent him to a summer camp for troubled teenagers. "Lee, we are doing this because we love you, and think that this camp will help you. When you come back, if you willingly fit in and uphold your responsibilities in the family, we will meet you halfway. But if you insist on rebelling against your life here, we will have to send you back," they told him.

Bill and Susan had deep convictions from the Bible about what God required of them as parents. Through all the heartache, they stuck to their guns. The change was not dramatic, but slowly, as Lee grew to maturity, the impact of Bill and Susan's unconditional love and consistent discipline brought its reward. Lee began to see the futility of his way of life, and the deep richness of Bill and Susan's. He changed from the inside out, and committed his life to Christ.

A man now, Lee is happy, polite, quiet, gentle, disciplined, responsible, courteous, and friendly. The transformation is remarkable. And make no mistake about it. Lee understands his incredibly good fortune in being adopted by Bill and Susan and the remarkable transformation they brought about. He practically worships the ground they walk on. When they are together, security, purpose, meaning, belonging, happiness, joy, warmth, and laughter mark their relationship. Bill and Susan delight in Lee. Lee enjoys Bill and Susan, and the more Lee becomes like Bill and Susan, the more he enjoys them.

To enjoy God forever is a concept beyond our full comprehension. It does not mean enjoying God as you would a rollercoaster ride, or a new car, or a job promotion. But it surely includes enjoying God by becoming less like what He isn't, and more like what He is. When we experience or imagine the best friendships or "loves" on earth, I think we glimpse how we will enjoy God in heaven forever. Unity, meaning, purpose, love, acceptance, and belonging characterize the relationship. It never wears thin, it never grows stale. When God fills the deepest longings of our soul, we can enjoy Him, and that, forever.

What Is the Focus of the Old Testament?

The Old Testament focuses on the temporary solution God provided to humanity's sin problem.

Sin, and only sin, separates and alienates humanity from God and prevents our enjoying Him. Therefore, the sin problem needs to be dealt with to reconcile humanity to God. Humanity must find a way for its sin to be forgiven. God Himself provided His sinless Son to die in our place, so that Jesus' death could count for ours, Jesus' life could be given to us, and Jesus' righteousness attributed to us. Of course, Jesus the Son was not given to us until New Testament times. During the time of the Old Testament, God established a system of sacrifice and worship that pictured or foreshadowed the reality to come. In this way He demonstrated to the world through Israel that He was who He said He was.

Unconfessed sin keeps us from enjoying God.

Separation from God through sin is called "death" (Romans 6:23). God pictured this spiritual reality in the Old Testament through a system of animal sacrifice. It is important to understand what the sacrificial system did and what it did not do. The prophet Samuel said, ". . . to obey is better than sacrifice, / And to heed than the fat of rams" (1 Samuel 15:22 NASB). David said in Psalm 51:16–17, "You do not desire sacrifice, or else I would give it; / You do not delight in burnt offering. The sacrifices of God are a broken spirit, / A broken and a contrite heart— / These, O God, You will not despise."

Merely sacrificing animals to God does not take away sins. God requires repentance in order to forgive sins. Jesus called the Pharisees in the New Testament "white-washed sepulchers" because they kept up the proper appearance on

Animal sacrifices reminded people graphically of sin's true cost—death.

the outside, but inside they were unrepentant. But if you were repentant, God prescribed sacrifices which you were to offer. These, always costly, usually included the death of an animal, which portrayed actual death. They reminded people graphically of the true cost and consequences of sin. The physical picture simulated the spiritual and ultimate result of sin—eternal death.

This visual aid helps us understand what was at stake with our sin and what it would take in order for us to have our sins forgiven permanently. If we did not want to have to offer animal sacrifices throughout eternity, something had to happen permanently to remove the need. That "something" was the sacrificial death of Jesus, upon which the New Testament focuses.

What is the Focus of the New Testament?

The New Testament focuses on the permanent solution God has provided in Christ to humanity's sin problem.

What the Old Testament pictured, the New Testament presents in reality. In the Old Testament, sacrificed lambs covered the sins of Israel temporarily until they could be taken away permanently. In the New Testament, the Lamb of God, Jesus, was sacrificed so that all sins could be forgiven permanently. Jesus' death, entirely adequate to take away the sins of the whole world, actually affects only those who accept His offer of forgiveness, repent of their sins, and follow Him. Jesus meant, when He said that He had "fulfilled" the law, that no longer was it necessary to keep sacrificing bulls and goats and sheep. Now humanity needed only to rely on the Great Sacrifice of Calvary.

The message in the New Testament has nothing to do with sacrificing animals but with believing in Jesus. Jesus Himself commissioned His disciples to "Go, therefore, and make disciples of all the nations, baptizing them in the name of the Father and of the Son and of the Holy Spirit, teaching them to observe all things that I have commanded you; and lo, I am with you always, even to the end of the age" (Matthew 28:19–20). Jesus wants Christians to commit themselves to spreading the message of salvation by grace through faith in Him to everyone in the world.

Conclusion

Let me draw the loose ends together in summary. The message of the Bible is that God continuously demonstrates to the universe through us that He is who He says He is. He is perfect in moral character and unlimited in His ability to do what He chooses. The perfection of His moral character does not allow Him to ignore sin, yet it propels Him to offer the ultimate sacrifice Himself in order to provide a way for us to escape the penalty of our sin. His immeasurable power executes His plan that provides for our escape. In addition, as Packer said, God wants to make friends with us. He wants to be in a close relationship with us, finding His joy in giving us gifts and we finding our joy in giving Him our worship and thanks. That is God's end for us. Friendship between two persons has no further motive. It is an end in itself. It almost sounds too good to be true! In fact some have suggested that, not only is the chief end of man to glorify God *and* enjoy Him forever, but rather, our chief end is to glorify God *by* enjoying Him forever. *That* is good news! That is the Bible's message.

Speed Bump!

Q1. What is the message of the Bible?

A1. The message of the Bible is that God is *demonstrating* to the universe through us that He is who He says He is.

Q2. What is the focus of the Old Testament?

A2. The Old Testament focuses on the *temporary* solution God provided to humanity's sin problem.

Q3. What is the focus of the New Testament?

A3. The New Testament focuses on the *permanent* solution God has provided in Christ to humanity's sin problem.

Fill in the Blank

Question
Answer

Q1. What is the message of the Bible?

A1. The message of the Bible is that God is _____ to the universe through us that He is who He says He is.

Q2. What is the focus of the Old Testament?

A2. The Old Testament focuses on the _____ solution God provided to humanity's sin problem.

Q3. What is the focus of the New Testament?

A3. The New Testament focuses on the _____ solution God has provided in Christ to humanity's sin problem.

For Further Thought and Discussion

1. God is demonstrating to the universe through you that He is who He says He is. Specifically, in your life, what characteristics of God can you identify that He has demonstrated to the universe through you?

2. In what ways in your own life have you come to "enjoy" God as a result of becoming more like Him?

3. God wants us to tell others about what He has done for us so that others might trust in Him also. If someone asked you to tell them what God has done for you and how they could become a Christian, what would you tell them?

What If I Don't Believe?

Unless I understand that God is demonstrating to the universe through me that He is who He says He is, I am limited in my understanding of the

Bible and what God has actually done for me. Because of my imperfect understanding, I have deficient gratitude and a diminished ability to worship God. I am hampered in my ability to understand the spiritual message of the Bible, and may confine my knowledge of the Bible to its stories and the do's and don'ts. My joy will not be full until I understand how completely God has committed Himself to my personal welfare.

For Further Study

1. Scripture

- Ephesians 1
- Hebrews 9:12–15
- Hebrews 10:1–18
- Hebrews 10:19–25
- Matthew 28:19–20

2. Books

Some other books helpful in studying this subject are listed below in general order of difficulty. If I could read only one of them, I would read the first one.

> *Desiring God*, John Piper
> *Authentic Christianity*, Ray Stedman
> *Rediscovering Holiness*, James I. Packer

Defend the Bible? I would just as soon defend a lion. Just turn the Bible loose. It will defend itself.
■ Charles H. Spurgeon

What Is God's Strategy for Relating to Humanity?

In ancient Persia, coming unbidden into the presence of the king could cost you your life. The book of Esther in the Old Testament tells the story of a young Jewish girl who becomes queen of Persia without the king's knowing her ancestry. When an unscrupulous manipulator named Haman hatches a plot to kill all the Jews in the kingdom, Esther realizes that she must talk to her husband. To come into his presence unbidden, however, could only result in one of two consequences: the king could extend his golden scepter in welcome, or withhold it in rejection. A withheld scepter brought the death penalty.

After Esther decided that she must appeal to the king to try to foil this plot, she said to her loved ones ". . . gather all the Jews . . . and fast for me; neither eat nor drink for three days, night or day. My maids and I will fast likewise. And so I will go to the king, which is against the law; and if I perish, I perish!" (Esther 4:16).

In this chapter we learn that . . .

1. Four main elements comprise God's strategy for relating to humanity: revelation, faith, blessing, and reproduction.
2. God worked through the nation of Israel, promising earthly reward for trusting obedience.
3. God worked through the church, promising spiritual reward for trusting obedience.
4. Our faithful obedience to God results in God's glory, our blessing, and a witness to the world.

Esther did not perish, but the chasm between monarch and subject has always been difficult and dangerous to cross. If daunting protocols surround mortal kings, how then does one approach God? On what basis might we be accepted into His presence and establish a relationship with Him? How can we be properly related to God?

In one sense, God is a monarch and certain rules apply to our approaching him. Yet, unlike most monarchs, God earnestly desires our fellowship. He encourages us to come to him. Billy Graham, in his book, *How To Be Born Again*, tells an interesting story which illustrates this so well:

> Picture a courtroom. God the Judge is seated in the judge's seat, robed in splendor. You are arraigned before Him. He looks at you in terms of His own righteous nature as it is expressed in the moral law. He speaks to you:
>
> God: John (or) Mary, have you loved Me with all your heart?
>
> John/Mary: No, Your Honor.
>
> God: Have you loved others as you have loved yourself?
>
> John/Mary: No, Your Honor.
>
> God: Do you believe you are a sinner and that Jesus Christ died for your sins?
>
> John/Mary: Yes, Your Honor.
>
> God: Then your penalty has been paid by Jesus Christ on the cross and you are pardoned. . . . Because Christ is righteous, and you believe in Christ, I now declare you legally righteous. . . .

Can you imagine what a newspaperman would do with this event?

SINNER PARDONED—
GOES TO LIVE WITH JUDGE

It was a tense scene when John and Mary stood before the Judge and had the list of charges against them read. However, the Judge transferred all of the guilt to Jesus Christ, who died on a cross for John and Mary. After John and Mary were pardoned, the Judge invited them to come to live with Him forever. The reporter on a story like that would never be able to understand the irony of such a scene, unless he had been introduced to the Judge beforehand and knew His character.

Pardon and Christ's righteousness come to us only when we totally trust ourselves to Jesus as our Lord and Savior. When we do this,

God welcomes us into His intimate favor. Clothed in Christ's righteousness we can now enjoy God's fellowship. (118–119)

Faith is the key to a relationship with God. If we believe in Him, He adopts us as His spiritual child. The relationship we might imagine existing between a model earthly father and child is a picture of the spiritual relationship we then have with God.

What Is God's Strategy for Relating to Humanity?

Four main elements comprise God's strategy for relating to humanity: revelation, faith, blessing, and reproduction.

1. God Reveals Truth to Humanity

In the earliest days, He revealed truth directly, through one-on-one contact, dreams and visions, or angel messengers, and so on. Now, He reveals truth primarily through the Bible.

2. God Asks People To Live by Faith

Many things which God asks take people in the opposite direction of their natural inclinations. They will respond only if they believe God. Such is the nature of faith. You believe something you can't see. You act on something contrary to your nature. You subordinate your own instincts to Someone who you believe has greater wisdom.

3. God Blesses the Faithful

As individuals live for God by faith, trusting God and obeying Him as best they know how, God blesses them, and gives them a deeply satisfying quality of life.

4. Others Desire To Know God

Finally, when others look at the Christian and see the blessing that comes to him through his relationship with God, they become thirsty to know God also.

These principles worked themselves out in the Old Testament differently than they did in the New Testament. We will look at each of these principles (revelation, faith, blessing, and reproduction) and see how they functioned in the Old and New Testaments.

How Was God's Strategy for Relating to Humanity Executed in the Old Testament?

God worked through the nation of Israel, promising earthly reward for trusting obedience.

Revelation

God revealed Himself to people in the Old Testament in different ways. In the era before Scripture, God used miraculous means, but after portions of the Old Testament were recorded, the people had the benefit of Scripture.

This revelation required the Old Testament people to act in ways that departed from normal behavior. For example, they were not to amass horses as military resources. God promised to protect them from all enemies and fight for them as long as they remained righteous.

They were to refrain from labor or commerce every seventh day. Every seventh year, they were to let their land lie fallow to rest it. God promised to bless their business and agricultural pursuits to such an extent that they would have plenty even throughout that seventh year.

They were to give almost thirty percent of their income in tithes and offerings for national taxes and for the functioning of the sacrificial and priestly systems. God promised to prosper them economically if they would obey these commands, so that they would be fabulously wealthy.

Faith

If you believed that an invisible God would protect you from enemies, you would be willing to forego the development of a cavalry and chariots for warfare. If you did not trust God to protect you, you would disobey and raise all the horses you could to protect yourself.

If you believed that an invisible God would prosper your farming to such an extent that you could actually not plant one year out of seven, and spend that year in praise to the Lord, you would obey, and forego planting the seventh year. If you did not trust God to prosper you, you would disobey, and raise all the crops you could to supply yourself.

If you believed that God would prosper you financially, so that you could afford to give thirty percent of your money for national and religious purposes, you would obey and tithe your income. If you didn't trust God to prosper you, you would disobey, and keep the money for yourself.

Why I Need to Know This

I need to know this because I might otherwise misunderstand how God works in my life. I might think that some Old Testament blessings should be coming to me as a result of my faithful obedience to God, or fear that God is displeased with me for something that I don't know about. I might expect things from God that He hasn't promised a New Testament believer. I also need to know how God links revelation, faith, and blessing to the evangelization of the world. What I believe matters, but so does how I live.

These three examples illustrate how God's revelation took man in the opposite direction from his natural inclinations to protect himself, supply himself, and fund himself. Faith requires that you believe God and do things His way.

Blessing

God blesses living by faith.

If the Israelites would trust God to meet their needs, and obey His commandments, God promised to give them, not just subsistence, but abundance beyond comprehension in every area of their national life.

Now it shall be, if you will diligently obey the LORD your God, being careful to do all His commandments which I command you today, the LORD your God will set you high above all the nations of the earth. And all these blessings shall come upon you and overtake you, if you will obey the LORD your God.

Blessed shall you be in the city, and blessed shall you be in the country. Blessed shall be the offspring of your body and the produce of your ground and the offspring of your beasts, the increase of your herd and the young of your flock. Blessed shall be your basket and your kneading bowl. Blessed shall you be when you come in, and blessed shall you be when you go out.

The LORD will cause your enemies who rise up against you to be defeated before you; they shall come out against you one way, and shall flee before you seven ways. The LORD will command the blessing upon you in your barns and in all that you put your hand to, and He will bless you in the land which the LORD your God gives you.

The LORD will establish you as a holy people to Himself, as He swore to you, if you will keep the commandments of the LORD your God, and walk in His ways. So all the peoples of the earth shall see that you are called by the name of the LORD, and they shall be afraid of you (Deuteronomy 28:1–10 NASB).

God put His word on the line in unambiguous terms. Marvelous blessing would be theirs if they wholeheartedly obeyed His commandments.

Reproduction

God did not choose the nation of Israel to the exclusion of all other peoples. He chose Israel in order to reach all nations. God's idea was to so bless Israel that the world would see the thumbprint of God on their national life, and desire to know their God because of the quality of life He had given Israel.

Psalm 67 states this succinctly:

God be gracious to us and bless us,
And cause His face to shine upon us—
That Thy way may be known on the earth,
Thy salvation among all nations.
Let the peoples praise Thee, O God;
Let all the peoples praise Thee.
Let the nations be glad and sing for joy.
For Thou wilt judge the peoples with uprightness,
And guide the nations on the earth.
Let the peoples praise Thee, O God;
Let all the peoples praise Thee.
The earth has yielded its produce;
God, our God, blesses us.
God blesses us,
That all the ends of the earth may fear Him (Psalm 67:1–7 NASB).

God always ties blessing to obedience to His commands. There it is in black and white. God blesses Israel that all the ends of the earth may fear (respect or reverence) Him.

God always tied blessing to obedience to His commandments. Israel, however, never succeeded in living righteously for very long. The longest sustained period of righteousness for the nation overlapped David's and the first part of Solomon's reigns, a period of perhaps 60 years. It resulted in the period of greatest national blessing. This stupendous era noticeably affected the surrounding nations.

We read in 1 Kings 10 that word of the splendor of Israel and the wisdom of Solomon spread, even to the queen of Sheba. So fascinated was she by the reports of Israel's grandeur that she came for a closer look. Solomon displayed to her his palace, the city of Jerusalem, and the temple, one of the most glorious buildings ever built.

After the queen had seen everything, the Bible says in verse 5 that "there was no more spirit in her." In other words, she swooned! "It was a true report which I heard in my own land about your words and your wisdom," she said. "Nevertheless, I did not believe the reports until I came and my eyes had seen it. And behold, the half was not told me. You exceed in wisdom and prosperity the report which I heard."

Then she broke out in spontaneous eulogy to God. "Blessed be the LORD your God . . ." (1 Kings 10:6–9 NASB).

This was the way it was supposed to work. The people of the world see the splendor of Israel, and their attention is drawn to God.

How Was God's Strategy for Relating to Humanity Executed in the New Testament?

God worked through the church, promising spiritual reward for trusting obedience.

God's dealings with the nation of Israel were very much physical, and were designed to picture or foreshadow the spiritual truths which would be presented in the New Testament. The Old Testament sacrificial system foreshadowed in literal terms the spiritual work which would be done by Christ on the cross in the New Testament. The beauty of the Temple portrayed the glory of God. The physical blessing of protection and food depicted the spiritual protection and nourishment which is ours in Christ.

The blessings in the Old Testament were conspicuously material and physical—the fruit of the vine—although these by no means ruled out spiritual blessings for which the Psalms give earnest praise. The blessings in the New Testament are conspicuously spiritual—the fruit of the spirit, although material blessings are not ruled out.

Revelation

The revelation from God in the New Testament differs from that in the Old Testament. Christ said that He came to fulfill the Law. Now that He has come and died for our sins and has risen again from the dead, the sacrificial system and the observance of the Mosaic Law are no longer needed. For example, we no longer refrain from planting during the seventh year as we did in the physical kingdom because the physical kingdom has been superseded by the spiritual kingdom it represented.

Nevertheless, the nature of the revelation remains the same. It asks us to function in a way contrary to our natural inclinations: To keep our life, we must lose it; to be great, we must become servants; to be strong, we must be gentle. It is better to give than to receive. Pursue the kingdom of God first, and all our material needs will be met. Reality in the New Testament resides in the invisible, while that which is visible may often deceive us. We must live for the next world instead of this one. As C. S. Lewis said, when we shoot for the next world, we get this one too; but if we shoot for this one, we lose them both.

Faith

To successfully and obediently go against our natural inclinations requires faith. If we believe that God will exalt us if we humble ourselves, then we try to refrain from competing with others. If we believe that the anger of man does not work the righteousness of God, then we work on giving our anger over to God as we trust in His sovereignty. If we believe that God will feed and clothe us (not in great abundance, as was promised in the Old Testament), then we will give sacrificially to spread the gospel. If we believe God, we obey His commands. If we don't, we don't. The opposite of obedience is not disobedience but unbelief. When we lack faith we disobey.

The opposite of obedience is not disobedience but unbelief.

Blessing

In the Old Testament, God blessed the Israelites with material abundance—the fruit of the vine. In the New Testament, God blesses the church with spiritual abundance—the fruit of the

Spirit: love, joy, peace, patience, kindness, goodness, faithfulness, gentleness, self-control (Galatians 5:22–23). When asked what they want out of life, most people will say, "I just want to be happy." To the happy person, life has meaning. The blessing promised to the faithful child of God in the New Testament far exceeds that: peace, love, joy.

Reproduction

In the Old Testament, God promised to raise Israel above the other nations of the world by bestowing material abundance. In the New Testament, He promised to elevate individual Christians above the world by pouring out spiritual blessing. "Let your light so shine before men in such a way that they may see your good works, and glorify your Father who is in heaven" (Matthew 5:16 NASB). "Do all things without grumbling or disputing; that you may prove yourselves to be blameless and innocent, children of God above reproach in the midst of a crooked and perverse generation, among whom you appear as lights in the world" (Philippians 2:14–15 NASB). Our inner spiritual overflow rather than our outer material wealth manifests God to the world.

When we live as we ought, our lives call attention to the Lord and encourage others to become Christians. "A new commandment I give to you, that you love one another, even as I have loved you, that you also love one another. By this all men will know that you are My disciples, if you have love for one another" (John 13:34–35 NASB). As Christ is accurately portrayed and proclaimed to the world, people will be drawn to Him to become Christians.

What Are the Consequences of Faithful Obedience to God?

Our faithful obedience to God results in God's glory, our blessing, and a witness to the world.

Our proper relationship to God centers on faith. Having faith is the only thing we can do, and still do nothing. It is the one response we can make and still not be responsible for saving ourselves.

By faith, we become God's spiritual children, and by faith we read His revelation, believe it, and respond accordingly. In doing so, we become eligible for His spiritual blessing, which has three primary consequences:

1. God is glorified. As we strive to live in trust and obedience to God according to the Scriptures, our lives gradually take on the character of God Himself. When this happens, the world gets an accurate picture of who God really is because it sees Him in us. The value and worth of God becomes publicly known, and in this way God is glorified.

2. Believers are satisfied. We who are His spiritual children experience the pleasure of the life which God grants us. Peace, love, and joy become ours in increasing measure even in the midst of life's unavoidable pain.

3. Others are evangelized. As people notice the quality of life available to the children of God, some will desire to know Jesus because of what they see of Him in our lives.

Conclusion

God wants to have a personal relationship with us. Our faith in Him establishes this relationship.

Revelation: He has given us His word, the Bible.

Faith: The Bible asks us to do some things against our natural inclinations. If we trust God and believe in Him, we do them. If we don't trust, we don't obey.

Blessing: If we believe God, and wholeheartedly obey the Bible, He blesses us with spiritual abundance.

Reproduction: If our lives exhibit the spiritual abundance of God, others will want to become Christians, too.

Speed Bump!

Question
Answer

Q1. What is God's strategy for relating to humanity?

A1. *Four* main elements comprise God's strategy for relating to humanity: revelation, faith, blessing, and reproduction.

Q2. How was God's strategy for relating to humanity executed in the Old Testament?

A2. God worked through the nation of Israel, promising *earthly* reward for trusting obedience.

Q3. How was God's strategy for relating to humanity executed in the New Testament?

A3. God worked through the church, promising *spiritual* reward for trusting obedience.

Q4. What are the consequences of faithful obedience to God?

A4. Our faithful obedience to God results in God's *glory*, our blessing, and a witness to the world.

Fill in the Blank

Question
Answer

Q1. What is God's strategy for relating to humanity?

A1. _____ main elements comprise God's strategy for relating to humanity: revelation, faith, blessing, and reproduction.

Q2. How was God's strategy for relating to humanity executed in the Old Testament?

A2. God worked through the nation of Israel, promising _____ reward for trusting obedience.

Q3. How was God's strategy for relating to humanity executed in the New Testament?

A3. God worked through the church, promising _____ reward for trusting obedience.

Q4. What are the consequences of faithful obedience to God?

A4. Our faithful obedience to God results in God's _____ , our blessing, and a witness to the world.

For Further Thought and Discussion

1. If the true test of our belief in the Bible is our obedience to it, what things in your life would you say you believe, though your actions demonstrate otherwise?

2. It takes time for our lives to change and for God's blessings to take root as a result, so we must be patient and wait for change. What main areas in your life are you still waiting to see changed?

3. In what areas have you seen blessing and change?

4. Have you had an opportunity to talk with someone about the Lord because they brought up a distinctive quality of your life or something you have done?

What If I Don't Believe?

If I don't believe God's strategy for relating to humanity, I can get mixed up on many different fronts. First, I may get confused and think that God is expecting something of me that He isn't (an Old Testament command), or that He should be blessing me for my obedience to an Old Testament promise. I may not see the link between my faithful obedience and God's blessing, and wonder why God isn't blessing me, even though I may be living an obedient life. I may not understand that my quality of life gives me credibility in sharing my faith with others.

For Further Study

1. Scripture

- Deuteronomy 28
- Psalm 67
- Romans 15:4
- 1 Corinthians 10:11
- Romans 16:27
- Galatians 5:22–23
- John 17:20–21

2. Books
30 Days to Understanding the Bible, Max Anders

This chapter was adapted from chapter 28 of *30 Days to Understanding the Bible* and used by permission of Word, Inc.

Scripture is like a pair of spectacles which dispels the darkness and gives us a clear view of God.
■ John Calvin

How Does the Bible Picture Itself?

If a picture is worth a thousand words, then the Bible is shorter than it could be by thousands of words because of all the marvelous word pictures in it. Not only did Jesus preach in word pictures (the good shepherd, the lost lamb, the lost coin, the lost son, and so on), but God, as He inspired the Bible, moved the authors to fill the Scriptures with vivid descriptions that help us understand and appreciate the truth within its pages. For example, the temporary system of animal sacrifice in the Old Testament depicts the permanent sacrifice which Jesus would make. Five word pictures used in Scripture help describe the Bible: a mirror, a sword, light, water, and food. We will explore each of these.

How Is the Bible Like a Mirror?
The Bible is like a mirror in that it accurately reflects our spiritual appearance.

In *Snow White and the Seven Dwarfs*, the wicked queen asks her enchanted mirror, "Mirror, mirror on the wall, who's the fairest one of all?" The mirror cannot lie. So for years it says, "You, O queen, are the fairest in the land." But one day, the queen asks, "Mirror, mirror on the wall, who's the fairest one of all?" and the mirror responds, "Snow White is the fairest of them all." The enraged queen decides to destroy Snow White. The plan fails, however. A handsome prince rescues Snow White and carries her away to live happily ever after.

Though only a fairy tale, the story is based on one fundamental truth. A mirror doesn't lie. If your nose is dirty, it tells you.

If your hair is a mess, it tells you. If your clothes don't fit, it tells you. Anything about your appearance that you want to know, you can ask a mirror. It will tell you the truth every time.

In James 1:22–25 we read:

But prove yourselves doers of the word, and not merely hearers who delude themselves. For if anyone is a hearer of the word and not a doer, he is like a man who looks at his natural face in a mirror; for once he has looked at himself and gone away, he has immediately forgotten what kind of person he was. But one who looks intently at the perfect law, the law of liberty, and abides by it, not having become a forgetful hearer but an effectual doer, this man shall be blessed in what he does. (NASB)

When we look into the word of God, we see what we look like and are admonished to correct anything that is out of place. It discloses attitudes that need adjustment. It tells us if our values are a mess. It bares our dirty thoughts. And just as we correct what we see wrong in a glass mirror, so we must, by the guidance and strength of the Holy Spirit, correct the defects the spiritual mirror reveals.

In this chapter we learn that . . .

1. The Bible is like a mirror in that it accurately reflects our spiritual appearance.
2. The Bible is like a sword in that it can be used as a weapon both to defend us and attack the enemy.
3. The Bible is like light in that it enables us to see in the darkness of life so that we stay on the right path and avoid harm.
4. The Bible is like water in that it quenches our thirst and cleanses us from spiritual impurities.
5. The Bible is like food in that it satisfies our spiritual hunger, and causes us to grow.

Perhaps we have been harboring resentment over a fellow worker who received the promotion and raise we had hoped for. We look into the mirror, and we read, "love does not envy" (1 Corinthians 13:4). Uh-oh. Later we read: "Bondservants [employees], obey in all things your masters [employers] according to the flesh, not with eyeservice, as men-pleasers, but in sincerity of heart, fearing God. And whatever you do, do it heartily, as to the Lord and not to men, knowing that from the Lord you will receive the reward of the inheritance; for you serve the Lord Christ" (Colossians 3:22–24). Ohhhh. The killer blow! Our attitude falls short of the word. We have no right to fume. We must give up the resentment.

Or, perhaps we are reliving our childhood **The Bible as a** through our child or children. We think that if **mirror never lies.** we had received more guidance as a child we would have achieved great things. So we will make sure that our child accomplishes what we never did. We drive our child to succeed. Our child must attain the honor roll like our neighbor's child. Our child must excel in athletics like our brother's child. Our child has to play the piano well, like our preacher's child. Our child should be good-looking like our fellow committee member's child. We try not to show it, but we are disappointed when it isn't true. We cause our child to feel loved conditionally, that he or she can never please us.

Then we read, "Fathers [parents], do not provoke your children, lest they become discouraged" (Colossians 3:21); "do not provoke your children to wrath, but bring them up in the training and admonition of the Lord (Ephesians 6:4); "train up a child in the way he should go, and when he is old he will not depart from it" (Proverbs 22:6).

Whoops! Our values are askew. They are a mess, and need to be cleaned up. We are exasperating our children, and they are becoming discouraged. We need to repent and line up our values according to the word.

Or maybe we have gotten careless in watching television and going to movies. "After all," we say, "if we are going to let some common swearing, a little skin, or a bit of violence keep us from watching something, there won't be much to watch. Besides, that stuff doesn't affect me. I already have my values formed. I don't agree with the language, the skin, and the violence, so I just mentally screen it out."

Then we read, "I will walk within my house in the integrity of my heart. I will set no worthless thing before my eyes" (Psalm 101:2–3 NASB). And "do not participate in the unfruitful deeds of darkness, but instead even expose them; for it is disgraceful even to speak of the things which are done by them in secret" (Ephesians 5:11–12 NASB). Then again, "Finally, brethren, whatever is true, whatever is honorable, whatever is right, whatever is pure, whatever is lovely, whatever is of good repute, if there is any excellence and if anything worthy of praise, let your mind dwell on these things" (Philippians 4:8 NASB).

Mmmmm. Well. What we've been watching won't do. Our thoughts are soiled. They are vicarious thoughts, but they are soiled and need to be cleaned up.

The mirror doesn't lie. We can live in denial and go away without heeding the word, but then we become the person who sees a dirty nose, ratty hair, and ill-fitting clothes yet does nothing about it, forgetting what he really looks like.

How is the Bible Like a Sword?

The Bible is like a sword in that it can be used as a weapon both to defend us and attack the enemy.

I will never forget seeing a karate expert give a demonstration of his skill. After breaking boards with his hands and cement blocks with his head, he asked for a volunteer from the audience. (Why would *anyone* volunteer for anything at a karate demonstration?) He had the volunteer (a macho teenage boy) lie down on his back, and the expert laid a watermelon on the boy's stomach. Then the karate expert took out a sword sharp enough to shave a thirteen-year-old's peach fuzz. This three-and-a-half-foot-long broadsword, gleamed spotlessly in the midday sun before bleachers full of anxious spectators. The powerfully built wielder of this death instrument raised it over his head with both hands. The only things between the boy and the blade was a plump watermelon and a T-shirt. The crowd held its breath. The sword flashed downward at a speed that would be missed if the eye blinked at the wrong moment. In a wink it pierced the top of the melon rind, sliced through the red pulp, split the bottom of the melon rind—and stopped precisely where melon met T-shirt. The two cleanly split halves of the watermelon dropped neatly to the floor. The young man got up with a humble, sheepish grin on his face that said, "If I had known what I was getting into, I would never have volunteered."

It was an astonishing display of precision. One inch too short, and the watermelon would not have been cut in half. One inch too far, and the teenager would have been disemboweled. A fifth-degree black belt in karate is trained to kill, if need be, with skill, precision, effectiveness, and safety to himself. If he is trained to use a sword, he knows how to wield it on a level that an untrained person cannot even imagine.

This gives us additional insight to a passage such as Hebrews 4:12, which reads:

> For the word of God is living and powerful, and sharper than any two-edged sword, piercing even to the division of soul and spirit, and of joints and marrow, and is a discerner of the thoughts and intents of the heart.

Just as a skilled swordsman is able to place his sword into a person's body at the exact point he chooses, so the word of God is able to pierce a person's soul and spirit at whatever precise point God elects.

Of course, the Holy Spirit applies the word of God to our needs. We read in 1 Corinthians 2:9–10, 12:

> "Eye has not seen, nor ear heard / Nor have entered into the heart of man / The things which God has prepared for those who love Him." But God has revealed them to us through His spirit. For the Spirit searches all things, yes, the deep things of God. . . . Now we have received, not the spirit of the world, but the Spirit who is from God, that we might know the things that have been freely given to us by God.

Why I Need To Know This

In knowing this I will more fully comprehend the richness of the Bible and the many ways I can apply it to my daily life. In understanding the word pictures used to describe the Bible, I can now read the Bible and use it as a mirror to show me what I am really like, or a sword to protect myself, or light to illuminate my way, or water to quench my spiritual thirst for answers to life's great questions, or food to grow by daily.

When we struggle through a trial or flounder under some weakness, the Holy Spirit directs the word of God to us in a way that cuts directly to the issue. Are you struggling with worry? The Holy Spirit will take a passage like Matthew 6 and cause it to jump up off the page:

> Which of you by worrying can add one cubit to his stature? . . . Therefore do not worry, saying, "What shall we eat?" or "What shall we drink?" or "What shall we wear?" For after all these

things the Gentiles seek. For your heavenly Father knows that you need all these things. But seek first the kingdom of God and His righteousness, and all these things shall be added to you. Therefore, do not worry about tomorrow, for tomorrow will worry about its own things. Sufficient for the day is its own trouble (vv. 27, 31–34).

If you are floundering under a weakness, the Holy Spirit will bring a passage alive to you such as 1 Corinthians 9:24–27:

Do you not know that those who run in a race all run, but only one receives the prize? Run in such a way that you may win. And everyone who competes in the games exercises self-control in all things. They then do it to receive a perishable wreath, but we an imperishable. Therefore I run in such a way, as not without aim; I box in such a way, as not beating the air; but I buffet my body and make it my slave, lest possibly, after I have preached to others, I myself should be disqualified. (NASB)

The Spirit applies the sword with pinpoint accuracy to our pressing need. As the Holy Spirit uses the word of God, so can we. We play it for both defense and protection. We brandish it in attack when we advance into enemy territory. Ephesians 6:17 calls the word of God the "sword of the Spirit," part of the spiritual armor described in that chapter, which protects us from the wiles of the devil, and enables us to stand firm against him.

Jesus thwarted Satan with the word. After fasting forty days, Jesus was hungry. The devil urged Him to turn stones into bread, which, for reasons that are not fully explained, would have been wrong. Jesus' reply was, "It is written, 'Man shall not live by bread alone, but by every word that proceeds from the mouth of God.' " The devil then goaded Jesus to perform a flamboyant miracle to prove He was the Son of God. Jesus replied, "It is written again, 'You shall not tempt the Lord your God.' " Finally, the devil offered to give Jesus all the kingdoms of the world if Jesus would worship him. Jesus said, "Away with you, Satan! For it is written, 'You shall worship the Lord your God, and Him only you shall serve.' " Then the devil left Him (see Matthew 4:1–11).

In each instance, Jesus routed the devil by quoting Scripture to him. In this way, Jesus withstood the temptations of the great deceiver and destroyer. I am persuaded that Jesus quoted these

Scriptures, not out of His omniscience as God, but because as a child He had memorized these passages, just as you and I have to memorize passages if we are to use them in similar circumstances. If Jesus used memorized Scripture to withstand the attacks of the enemy, how much more should we depend on the same strategy?

How Is the Bible Like Light?

The Bible is like light in that it enables us to see in the darkness of life so that we stay on the right path and avoid harm.

One of the wackier things I have done in my life is explore caves. I'm not particularly interested in exploring caves, but a friend of mine suggested it, and in a moment of shortsightedness I agreed. We were living in Atlanta at the time, and we drove to a little-known spot where Alabama, Georgia, and Tennessee meet, called Lymrock Blowing Cave. From a "blowing" cave a great rush of fifty-five-degree air blows out twenty-four hours a day. To keep us from opening our skulls on the sharp top of the cave when we came to low spots, we wore miner's helmets, hard hats with little lights on the top of them. The lights, of course, were to help us see. A remote cave lacks electrical switches.

A river flowed through this cave, and after walking upstream in the river, we came to a fork in the cave. Several forks later found us walking on solid ground. We left the river. Since my friend had made this trip several times before, I trusted him to know where we were going. Finally, the cave narrowed so that we had to squeeze ourselves through some passages. In fact, one spot was so narrow that I had to exhale and force myself through the passage into a larger space before I could inhale again. It is one of those things to brag about now, but one you would never get me to do again in a million years!

One thing that bothered me was the possibility of losing our light, even though we had our miner's helmets, a flashlight apiece, and plenty of batteries. We turned off our lights just to see what it would be like. Involuntarily, my eyelids reached for the ceiling and my eyes bugged like a bullfrog's. The total absence of light a half a mile back into a room in a cave that you had to squeeze yourself into is a level of darkness that I could not have comprehended without experiencing it. I put my hand in front of my eyes and waved it around to see if I could detect any motion. I couldn't. Then we turned our lights back on and walked out of the cave.

The Scriptures are a miner's helmet, a flashlight in a dark cave. The lights on our helmets were surprisingly weak. (The weaker the bulb, the longer the battery will last.) It didn't take much light to get out of the cave. But without the light, I am sure my bones would still be in that cave. No way in the world would we ever have gotten out of the cave without light. When you cannot see, you are an absolute victim to your surroundings. You don't know the turns, the holes, the breaks in the rock that lead you from room to room. Without light, you are lost, doomed to flounder and stumble, imprisoned by the elements, and destined to die in the darkness.

This experience gave new meaning to the passages, "The entrance of Your words gives light;" and "Your word is a lamp to my feet / And a light to my path." (Psalm 119:130, 105). The metaphor is clear. Ignorance of the word, ignorance of the truth, is darkness as black as the cave I was in. The Scriptures are a miner's helmet, a flashlight. A modern paraphrase of this passage might be, "Your word is a miner's helmet to my feet, and a flashlight to my path."

Without the Scriptures, we are victims of our surroundings. We don't know where to walk in life. We don't know which passages lead us to safety. We cannot see the pitfalls, the cliffs, the low headroom. We don't know when to turn right, when to turn left, when to keep walking straight. We cannot even walk straight, because without sight to guide us, we wander in circles.

The Scriptures help us see, prevent us from stepping into holes or walking off cliffs, and lead us to safety. If we will learn the Bible and commit ourselves to following it, then it is light to us in a dark world.

How Is the Bible Like Water?

The Bible is like water in that it quenches our thirst and cleanses us from spiritual impurities.

I know what it is like to be thirsty. On the farm baling hay during my summers in high school and later working my way through college on summer construction jobs that had me toiling on hot pavement, or on metal roofs or in holes with a pick and shovel, I would get so thirsty that I thought I would have to duct-tape a water hose to my mouth to quench it. One hot July day, with the temperature nearing 100 degrees, I was baling hay. Working without a shirt on, my body became slick with sweat. As I hiked the last bale onto the wagon high over my head, the chaff from the hay rained down on me like salt from a shaker that pours too fast, covering me with itchy bits of alfalfa, some of which lodged between my belt and my skin. I was so thirsty, I thought I would die. Visions of a lost soul crawling across an endless, mirage-filled desert danced in my mind. There and then I determined to go to college and graduate school as long as I needed, in order to get a job in an air-conditioned office in the summertime.

People who have been shipwrecked have been known to go insane because of thirst. The internal drive for water when the body needs it is intense.

I also know what it means to be spiritually thirsty. We thirst for meaning and purpose. We thirst to know who we are and why we are here. We thirst to know where we came from and where we are going. We thirst for meaningful relationships. And when we have wandered without sense and purpose, when we have gone too long without the answers to life's great questions, we develop a driving thirst that must be satisfied or our soul shrivels and dies.

Why I Need To Know This

I need to understand the word pictures of the Bible in order to grasp everything the Bible is intended to do for us. God purposed it to change our lives, affect every moment, and be the guiding truth of all we do.

During a time of intense spiritual thirst I came to Christ, Who is the Living Word of God (John 1:1, 14; Revelation 19:13). I had been longing for purpose and meaning, yearning to know what life was all about, and hoping for some assurance for life after death. My thirst drove me to seek God, and He gave me "living water" so that I would never have to thirst again. I learned who I was (a child of God), where I had come from (created by Him), why I was here (to know Him and make Him known), and where I was going (to live with God in heaven forever). Such wonder-

ful news was like a tall glass of cool, pure water on a sweltering
summer day. It soothed my parched throat, slaked my thirst, and
poured life into my soul.

**God's word slakes
our spiritual thirst.**
The "living water" image comes from the
Gospel of John, chapter four, in which Jesus is
talking with a woman at a well near Samaria in
the heat of the day. He asked the woman if she would give him a
drink of water. She wondered why Jesus, a Jew, would speak to a
Samaritan, since there was historic hatred between Jews and
Samaritans. Jesus said, "If you knew who you were talking to,
you would ask Him and He would give you living water, and
never thirst again." The woman found that living water that af-
ternoon, and never thirsted again. In that way, the word of God is
like water.

The word is also like water in that it cleanses us. We read in
Ephesians 5:25–26, "Husbands, love your wives, just as Christ
also loved the church and gave Himself for her, that He might
sanctify and cleanse her with the washing of water by the
word. . . ."

The word not only slakes our thirst, but also cleanses us.
When we sin, we read in 1 John 1:8–9, "If we say that we have no
sin, we deceive ourselves, and the truth is not in us. If we confess
our sins, He is faithful and just to forgive us our sins and to
cleanse us from all unrighteousness." The word, as a mirror,
shows us where the dirt (sin) is in our lives, and then the same
word, as water, cleanses us as we confess our sins. Life and
cleansing, two wonderful gifts of the word, are ways in which the
word is like water.

How Is the Bible Like Food?

*The Bible is like food in that it satisfies our spiritual hunger, and causes us
to grow.*

When I was working construction in college, not only did I
get very thirsty, I also got ravenously hungry. Hard work revved
up an already rapid metabolism to turbocharged speed. For
breakfast, I ate three eggs, a half-dozen slices of bacon, four pieces
of toast, a large glass of orange juice, and a big bowl or two of ce-
real. For lunch, which I carried in an ice chest instead of a lunch
box, I ate two big lunchmeat or meatloaf sandwiches, a sixteen-

ounce can of pears, peaches, or applesauce, a quart of milk and several packages of Twinkies, Ding-Dongs, or other such delicacies. My appetite astonished even me. Half an hour after eating a huge supper, I would saunter into the living room with a sixteen-ounce glass of milk and half a loaf of bread made up into peanut butter and jelly sandwiches. My mother still comments on that today. One of the great sources of relief in my adult life is that I don't have to feed anyone who eats like that.

The word of God nourishes eternal life and abundant life.

Hunger. A driving force, it demands to be filled just as does thirst. To satisfy that hunger, Jesus the Word of God, offers Himself to us again, this time as the Bread of Life:

Jesus answered them and said, "Truly, truly, I say to you, you seek Me, not because you saw signs, but because you ate of the loaves, and were filled. Do not work for the food which perishes, but for the food which endures to eternal life, which the Son of Man shall give to you, for on Him the Father, even God, has set His seal."

They said therefore to Him, "What shall we do, that we may work the works of God?"

Jesus answered and said to them, "This is the work of God, that you believe in Him whom He has sent."

They said therefore to Him, "What then do You do for a sign, that we may see, and believe You? What work do You perform? Our fathers ate the manna in the wilderness; as it is written, 'He gave them bread out of heaven to eat.' "

Jesus therefore said to them, "Truly, truly, I say to you, it is not Moses who has given you the bread out of heaven, but it is My Father who gives you the true bread out of heaven. For the bread of God is that which comes down out of heaven, and gives life to the world."

They said therefore to Him, "Lord, evermore give us this bread."

Jesus said to them, "I am the bread of life; he who comes to Me shall not hunger, and he who believes in Me shall never thirst (John 6:26–35 NASB).

The word is also called milk. Peter writes, "as newborn babes, desire the pure milk of the word, that you may grow thereby" (1 Peter 2:2 NASB).

The writer of the book of Hebrews writes:

For though by this time you ought to be teachers, you have need again for someone to teach you the elementary principles of the oracles of God, and you have come to need milk and not solid food. For everyone who partakes only of milk is not accustomed to the word of righteousness, for he is a babe. But solid food is for the mature, who because of practice have their senses trained to discern good and evil (Hebrews 5:12–14 NASB).

The Word of God gives us eternal life as well as abundant life. Jesus said, "I have come that they may have life, and that they may have it more abundantly" (John 10:10 NASB). The word sustains us, strengthens us, and encourages growth. It is the spiritual source of all that gives us life. In that way, the word of God has been pictured as food.

Conclusion

Both Jesus, the Living Word of God, and the Bible, the written word of God, are sources of life, providing the reflection of truth, the weapons of defense, light in darkness, water for our thirst, and food for our hunger.

Speed Bump!

*Q*uestion
*A*nswer

Q1. How is the Bible like a mirror?

A1. The Bible is like a mirror in that it accurately *reflects* our spiritual appearance.

Q2. How is the Bible like a sword?

A2. The Bible is like a sword in that it can be used as a *weapon* both to defend us and attack the enemy.

Q3. How is the Bible like light?

A3. The Bible is like light in that it enables us to *see* in the darkness of life so that we stay on the right path and avoid harm.

Q4.   How is the Bible like water?

A4.   The Bible is like water in that it quenches our *thirst* and cleanses us from spiritual impurities.

Q5.   How is the Bible like food?

A5.   The Bible is like food in that it satisfies our spiritual *hunger,* and causes us to grow.

Fill in the Blank

Question
Answer

Q1.   How is the Bible like a mirror?

A1.   The Bible is like a mirror in that it accurately _____ our spiritual appearance.

Q2.   How is the Bible like a sword?

A2.   The Bible is like a sword in that it can be used as a _____ both to defend us and attack the enemy.

Q3.   How is the Bible like light?

A3.   The Bible is like light in that it enables us to _____ in the darkness of life so that we stay on the right path and avoid harm.

Q4.   How is the Bible like water?

A4.   The Bible is like water in that it quenches our _____ and cleanses us from spiritual impurities.

Q5.   How is the Bible like food?

A5.   The Bible is like food in that it satisfies our spiritual _____ and causes us to grow.

For Further Thought and Discussion

1. In what ways have you seen, by learning the Scripture, an area of your life that needs change? What is the main area you think you should work on now?

2. In what ways have you realized that the Bible is like a sword in your life? What is the major application this truth has for your life today?

3. In what ways have you seen that the Bible is like light? What insight have you gained, or think you need to gain, in order to walk more securely in life?

4. In what ways have you noticed that the Bible is like water? How has the Scripture quenched your thirst? What is an area that still needs quenching?

5. In what ways have you seen that the Bible is like food? How has the Bible fed you? In what area do you still need to grow?

What If I Don't Believe?

If I accept the veracity of the Bible, there is not much to disbelieve here. If I don't believe that these word pictures of the Bible are true and applicable to my life, there are two problems. First, I miss out on the richness of understanding how the Bible can be used in my daily life. But even more seriously, I would be questioning the truth of the Scripture, which creates much greater problems which have been dealt with in earlier chapters.

For Further Study

1. Scripture

- Psalm 119:130
- Matthew 4:1–11
- John 6:26–35
- Ephesians 5:25–26
- Ephesians 6:17
- Hebrews 4:12
- James 1:22–25

2. Books
Other books helpful in studying this subject are listed below in general order of difficulty. If I could read only one, I would read the first one.

30 Days to Understanding the Bible, Max Anders
What the Bible Is All About, Henrietta C. Mears
God Has Spoken, James I. Packer

*Disregard the study of God and you sentence
yourself to stumble and blunder through life,
blindfolded, as it were, with no sense of
direction and no understanding of what
surrounds you.*
■ J. I. Packer

10

How Can We Study
the Bible Effectively?

In a 1977 interview in *Christianity Today*, Billy Graham was asked
what he would do differently if he had his life to live over again. He
replied, "One of my great regrets is that I have not studied enough. I
wish I had studied more and preached less. People have pressured me
into speaking to groups when I should have been studying and
preparing." Donald Barnhouse (pastor of the venerable Tenth Presbyterian Church in Philadelphia) said that if he knew the Lord was coming in three years, he would spend two of them studying and one
preaching. I am trying to make it up [study time] (*Taking the World's
Temperature* 19).

We all recognize the importance of Bible study, from the famous,
like Billy Graham, to the obscure little grandmother no one has ever
heard about. Even if we don't study our Bibles
diligently, we still usually think it is important.
But we don't have a very easy time of it when
we try it, and we easily become overwhelmed,
bored, or discouraged. There are probably several reasons why.

> **"I wish I had
> studied more and
> preached less,"**
> **—Billy Graham**

One explanation is that we study it in a vacuum. That is, we study
it without any specific need to use what we learn. A U.S. Army officer
once told of the contrast in his pupils during two different eras of
teaching at the artillery training school at Fort Sill, Oklahoma. In
1958–1960 the attitude was so lax that the instructors had a problem
getting the men to stay awake to listen. During the 1965–1967 classes,
however, the men hearing the same basic lectures were alert and took

copious notes. The reason: these men knew that in less than six weeks they would be facing the enemy in Vietnam. (Michael Green, *Illustrations for Biblical Preaching* 32).

Another reason that Bible study seems so irrelevant to many Christians is that they have no meaningful, spiritual interaction with non-Christians, no vital ministry to growing believers, and no personal and internal struggle for godliness, all of which bring the truths of the Bible to apply to life.

Most of the years I have been a Christian, I have *had* to study the Bible. I attended Christian institutions of higher education for twelve years after graduating from high school. Then I taught at a Christian college for several years. I eventually ended up pastoring and writing, which also forced me to study the Scriptures. However, during the years between teaching and pastoring in which I was not forced to study the Bible, I was a miserable failure at it. I have personally found it almost impossible to study the Bible consistently unless I place myself in a situation in which I must. It seems that many people are like me.

In this chapter we learn that . . .

1. The foundation for Bible study is spiritual rebirth, a desire to know the Bible, an obedient heart, and a plan to learn.

2. The three keys to Bible study are observation, interpretation, and application.

3. Observation is important, because unless we have observed correctly, we do not have reliable information.

4. We observe the Bible by developing a strategy that forces us to look closely at the text.

You don't have to get involved in the vocational ministry, however, to force yourself to study the Bible. There are other options. You might commit to a ministry, such as teaching Sunday school, visiting prisons, or joining an evangelism ministry at your church. You could join a Bible study group in your church or community. Often, that extra accountability to other people is enough to get you to do your lessons. Perhaps you and a friend could go through a book that will lead you into Bible study. Whatever the reason, if you are not one of the very few who is able to study your Bible consistently without an external

To succeed in Bible study, place yourself in a situation where you must study.

motivation, find some incentive that will work for you, and go for it. You will never regret becoming a better student of the Bible.

God's goal for us as Christians, while we are still on earth, is to change us into the character image of Jesus. The Bible, as applied to our hearts by the Holy Spirit, is His number-one tool. Romans 8:28 assures us "that in all things God works for the good of those who love Him, who have been called according to His purpose," which the next verse explains is "to be conformed to the likeness of His Son, that He might be the firstborn among many brothers" (Roman 8:28–29 NIV). Now that we are members of God's family, He desires us to increasingly take on "the family likeness."

How? Paul exhorted the believers in Rome, "Don't let the world around you squeeze you into its own mold, but let God re-make you so that your whole attitude is changed. Thus you will prove in practice that the will of God is good, acceptable to him and perfect" (Romans 12:2 PHILLIPS). God remolds our minds as we master, and are mastered by, His written word. This means more than just knowing the facts about God's character and actions. According to Hebrews 8:6–13, God's intent is to put His word in our minds and write it on our hearts by the Holy Spirit (v. 10). This is hard work. Scripture says:

> We have much to say about this [difficult subject], but it is hard to explain because you are slow to learn. In fact, though by this time you ought to be teachers, you need someone to teach you the elementary truths of God's word all over again. You need milk, not solid food! Anyone who lives on milk, being still an infant, is not acquainted with the teaching about righteousness. But solid food is for the mature, *who by constant use have trained themselves to distinguish good from evil* (Hebrews 5:11–14 NIV, emphasis added).

According to this text, to grow out of spiritual infancy into spiritual maturity we need to go into training!

What Is the Foundation for Bible Study?

The foundation for Bible study is spiritual rebirth, a desire to know the Bible, an obedient heart, and a plan to learn.

First, we have already seen in 1 Corinthians 2:14 that "the natural man (the non-Christian) does not receive the things of the Spirit of God, for they are foolishness to him; nor can he know them, because they are spiritually discerned." If a person isn't a Christian, he cannot grasp the spiritual truths of the Scripture. He can learn all about people, places, and events, but grasping the spiritual truths behind them and being changed by them is beyond him.

Second, the person must want to learn the Bible. The Bible claims to be the source of truth for living acceptably before God, and for ultimate meaning in life. God promises, to the person who walks in the spirit, the fruit of the Spirit: love, joy, peace, and more. If you had those three things, would you want anything else? What else is there?

Why I Need to Know This

If I don't realize that spiritual rebirth is a prerequisite for really understanding the Bible, I may try to study the Bible without being a Christian, and be very frustrated at its seeming lack of significance. If I don't know the fundamentals of observation, then even if I am a Christian, I am liable to be clumsy and ineffective in my attempts to study the Bible.

The question we must ask ourselves is, "Do we believe it?" We may say we believe many things, but our actions betray us. If we believed them we would act differently. By not studying the Bible, we indicate that we believe there is another avenue for a meaningful life. In fact, some of us have tried studying the Bible, and it was so hard, so boring, or so unyielding of anything significant, that life is easier not studying so hard. However, the question still comes back, do we believe the Bible? If we do, we have to believe that life can be lived more fully by being mature in the Scriptures than by being immature in the Scriptures. We must not allow ourselves the hypocritical position of saying that we believe the Bible to be the source of ultimate meaning in life, and then fail to study it.

Third, the person must cultivate obedience. If we decide to believe the Bible, then at some point in our life we must commit ourselves to seriously studying it. Three very crucial tests of a Christian's commitment face a person after accepting Jesus. The first is, when the Christian life becomes harder than one first thought it was going to be, "Am I going to commit myself totally to following Jesus, or am I going to do it half-heartedly?" The second one is, "Am I going to accept the Great Commission (Jesus' command to take the message of salvation by grace through faith in Christ to the whole world—Matthew 28:19–20) as my own personal commission, and do what I can to further it?" The third one is, "Am I going to become a serious student of the Bible?" Unless we face these three tests squarely and answer yes, we usually play around at Christianity.

Fourth in the foundation is developing a plan to learn the Bible. Most of us work hard to gain the knowledge and skills we need for success in careers, personal relationships, or various sports or hobbies. Success at anything worthwhile takes time and effort. We should not be surprised that the spiritual realm is no different. In fact, Paul urged Timothy: ". . . train yourself to be godly. For physical training is of some value, but godliness has value for all things, holding promise for both the present life and the life to come" (1 Timothy 4:7–8 NIV). Learning the Bible well is no easier than getting in excellent physical shape. But in the end, the rewards are greater.

Success in Bible study takes time and effort.

So what's our method? We can't join a Bible spa and work out every night after work. So what can we do? What method do we use? A method involves specific steps taken in a prescribed order to reach a definite goal.

What Are the Three Keys to Bible Study?

The three keys to Bible study are observation, interpretation, and application.

Effective Bible study involves three steps carried out in a prescribed order.

Observation of the text comes first. The key question here is "What does it say?" You immerse yourself in the text. Like a good detective, you note and list the details and relationships you see for further thought and comparison.

The second step is **interpretation**. At this point you attempt to answer the question "What does it mean?" The student tries to determine the author's purpose, thoughts, attitudes, and emotions. How would the original recipients have understood the message?

The final step is **application**. The pertinent question is "What does it mean to me?" In other words, how should my life change as a result of what God says in this passage? As Howard

Hendricks has said, "The Bible was not given to make us more intelligent sinners, but to change our lives." The Bible is the Word of God; as such, it demands an obedient and appropriate response.

Why Is Observation of the Bible So Important?

Observation is important, because unless we have observed correctly, we do not have reliable information.

Some people feel that observation wastes time. However, Oletta Wald asserts:

> The first skill you need to develop is to train your mind to *see* when you read a passage—to observe carefully the words, to be on the alert for details. Too many of us are in the habit of reading Scripture without seeing very much, without thinking about the words we are seeing. We read words, but we do not observe what the words are saying. Sometimes we do not even see all the words in a passage. We are lazy observers! Because of inaccurate and careless observations, we often make faulty interpretations and shallow applications (*The Joy of Discovery in Bible Study*, revised edition 16).

Howard Hendricks, who has taught personal Bible study to seminary students for over forty years, comments:

> Observation will give you the basic building blocks out of which you will construct the meaning of a passage. The answers to your questions will come directly from the observation process.
>
> That is why I say, the more time you spend in Observation, the less time you will need to spend in Interpretation, and the more accurate will be your results. The less time you spend in Observation, the more time you will need to spend in Interpretation, and the less accurate will be your results (*Living by the Book* 39).

The task of the observer is detection. If Sherlock Holmes had not been a careful observer, he wouldn't have solved a single case. He unraveled mysteries by seeing things others didn't. He noticed small details whose significance was missed by others, then drew inferences which cracked the case.

Studying the Bible is much the same. Although all Scripture is inspired of God and beneficial to us (2 Timothy 3:15–16), in one

sense we are "reading someone else's mail." Each book of the
Bible was written over 1,900 years ago in one or more non-
English languages to address specific situations
and questions. We lack a firsthand acquaintance **Careful observation**
with the authors and the recipients. So when **lays the foundation**
studying a particular text we need to accurately **for good Bible**
and fully notice the details, discerning what is **study.**
important and what is not.

Careful observation requires the purpose, patience, and
diligence illustrated in a New York *Times* advertisement for
Mortimer Adler's *How to Read a Book*. Beneath the picture of a
perplexed teenager poring over a letter were these words:

How to Read a Love Letter

This young man has just received his first love letter. He may have
read it three or four times, but he is just beginning. To read it as accurately as he would like, would require several dictionaries and
a good deal of close work with a few experts of etymology and
philology.

However, he will do all right without them.

He will ponder over the exact shade of meaning of every
word, every comma. She has headed the letter, "Dear John." What,
he asks himself, is the exact significance of these words? Did she
refrain from saying "Dearest" because she was bashful? Would
"My Dear" have sounded too formal?

Jeepers, maybe she would have said "Dear So-and-So" to anybody!

A worried frown will now appear on his face. But it disap-
pears as soon as he really gets to thinking about the first sentence.
She certainly wouldn't have written that to anybody!

And so he works his way through the letter, one moment
perched blissfully on a cloud, the next moment huddled miser-
ably behind an eight-ball. It has started a hundred questions in his
mind. He could quote it by heart. In fact, he will—to himself for
weeks to come (quoted in Robert A. Traina, *Methodical Bible Study*
97–98).

The advertisement concluded, "If people read books with
anything like the same concentration, we'd be a race of mental
giants." And if Christians read the Bible, God's love letter to
us, with the same concentration, we would be a race of spiritual
giants.

How Can We Observe the Bible?

We observe the Bible by developing a strategy that forces us to look closely at the text.

Yogi Berra was a catcher with the world champion New York Yankees years ago. Three times Most Valuable Player in the league, he later became a manager and led the Yankees to the World Series Championship. He is in the Baseball Hall of Fame, and everyone agrees he is a baseball genius. But if there were also a malapropism hall of fame, he would be a charter member. Don't know what a malapropism is? Listen: (speaking of the game of baseball, Yogi said) "Ninety percent of this game is half mental!" That's a malapropism (a comical confusion of words)! And his brain was either wired or unwired to be able to fire these things off at the speed of speech:

- A nickel ain't worth a dime anymore.
- Mickey Mantle's (one of baseball's greatest hitters) a switch hitter because he's amphibious.
- Slump? I ain't in no slump. I just ain't hitting.
- You give a hundred percent in the first half of the game, and if it isn't enough, in the second half, you give what's left.
- You got to be careful if you don't know where you're going, because you might not get there.
- What makes a great baseball manager, you ask? The answer is, a great baseball team!

Oh, Yogi! How do you do it?

I brought all this up because he said something else useful to us now: "You can see a lot just by looking." Ain't it the truth? In his own garbled way, he's talking about the need to observe carefully. You really can see a lot if you just look carefully.

To start your observations, get a pencil and paper. Because you would otherwise remember only a small number of your observations, write them down, whether in your study Bible, in a notebook, or in your computer. To get an idea of the overall picture, first read the book through in its entirety. For beginners you might want to pick a smaller book (three to five chapters is a good size).

1. Use the Six Basic Questions

Rudyard Kipling once wrote,

> I keep six honest serving men
> (They taught me all I knew);
> Their names are What and Why and When
> And How and Where and Who.

When determining what to observe, the six basic questions are always helpful.

Who is the author? To whom is he writing? List all the people involved. List anything that strikes you about a character.

What happened and in what order? What ideas are presented?

Where did this take place? What are the characteristics of the geographic setting? Where are the recipients? (Study with a map and every time a place is mentioned, look it up on the map.) Information will come alive if you do this!

Focus your observation with the six basic questions.

When did the events in the text take place? When did they occur in relation to other events in Scripture and in secular history? When was the writer writing? You may need a Bible history book in order to answer these questions.

Why does a particular person do or say something? Why is a particular "teaching" presented?

How are things accomplished? How well? By what method?

2. Note Key Terms

Look for key *terms*, those words that seem most important for understanding the passage. Repetition of a term, phrase, or clause is often a good clue as to what the author is attempting to communicate. For example, the word "believe" appears 79 times in John's Gospel and is critical to an understanding of its message. In fact, John asserts that his purpose in recording certain miraculous signs was "that you may believe that Jesus is the Christ, the Son of God, and that believing you may have life in His name" (John 20:31). Similarly, the repetition of "do not worry" or "do not be anxious" gives a strong indication as to Jesus' thrust in Matthew 6:25–34. One cannot understand Paul's excellent summary of the gospel message in Romans 3:21–26 apart from such terms as "law," "the Law," "righteousness," "faith," "sin," "grace," "justify," "redemption," and "sacrifice of atonement."

3. Identify the Structure

Hendricks and Hendricks suggest the student look for five different kinds of literary structure (The following is summarized from *Living By the Book*, pp. 118–119).

Authors of narratives frequently use **biographical structure** as they focus on key individuals in their stories.

A book's structure tells you how its parts merge to accomplish its purpose.

For example, Genesis 12–50 shifts the spotlight in turn to four generations of family leaders: Abraham, Isaac, Jacob, and Joseph. The book of Judges is structured around the various leaders known as judges who God raised up during the period between Joshua and Samuel.

In **geographical structure** the focus is on place. To understand the structure of Exodus the reader must note the various places that the nation of Israel visits as it travels from Egypt to the Promised Land.

Historical structure is based on the key events. The book of Joshua is built upon the reporting of different events. The Lord commissions Joshua to lead the people into the Promised Land after the death of Moses. Spies are sent out for reconnaissance. Israel crosses the Jordan. Jericho falls. Due to Achan's sin the Israelites initially experience defeat at Ai. And so on as they conquer the land.

Chronological structure, emphasizing key times, is closely related to historical structure. Narratives usually proceed in this way. The temporal progression of events is often signaled by connectives such as "after," "before," "meanwhile," "now," "since," "then," "until," "when," "whenever," and "while."

Ideological structure is organized around key ideas and concepts. Most of the epistles are developed in this way. Once you determine the central purpose, it is relatively easy to outline the book because you can see how each part contributes to that purpose. For example, many of the books of the New Testament begin with the presentation of spiritual and doctrinal truth. The rest of the book talks about how our lives should be changed by that truth.

The first three chapters of Ephesians are spent talking about how God has provided a way for us to be saved from our sins through Christ, and that this salvation is by grace through faith in Him. The last three chapters are spent talking about how the Ephesian believers ought to be living in light of the things that

God has already done for them. The transition from one part to the other is Ephesians 4:1, which says, "I, therefore, the prisoner of the Lord, beseech you to walk worthy of the calling with which you were called." In the first three chapters, Paul explained "the calling" with which they were called. Then, he says, "live worthy of your calling." This is a very common example of structure, especially in the epistles.

Structural relationships or patterns help you understand a passage. Note the use of comparisons and contrasts. *Comparisons* show how things are alike. Connectives used to indicate comparisons include "also," "as," "even so," "just as . . . so," "like," "likewise," and "too." For example, in James 3:3–5 the tongue is compared to the bit in a horse's mouth, a ship rudder, and a spark that starts a forest fire. *Contrasts* show how things differ. Sample connectives include "although," "but," "however," "much more," "nevertheless," and "yet." Galatians 5:19–23 contrasts the deeds of the flesh with the fruit of the Spirit.

The potential importance of *repetition* has been alluded to earlier in the discussion of key terms. Authors can also signal what is important to them by repeating characters, circumstances, patterns, and other Scripture. Be alert to *proportion*, which indicates the importance of something by the amount of space the author devotes to different subjects or periods of time. For example, Genesis devotes only 11 chapters to the comparatively lengthy period from creation to Abraham and 39 chapters to Abraham and the next three generations of his family (Isaac, Jacob, and Joseph). This coverage signals the author's narrowed focus on the family God chose to be His instrument of blessing to all peoples (Genesis 12:1–3).

4. Identify the Literary Form

Determining literary form is important in reading any piece of literature. There are several kinds of literature in the Bible. Historical books tell stories. Poetical books give us poetry and song. Prophetical books foretell the future and speak God's will forcefully. Epistles, which are letters to churches or individuals, instruct us in practical daily living based on biblical truth.

You will not see the things in poetry that you do in history. In history the "who, what, why, when, where, and how" are expressed in a sequence that the writer believes will help the audience see the points the writer wants to make, which usually focus on explaining divine and human action. Those questions usually aren't expressed or answered in the same way in poetry. So be aware that some methods of observation work better on some kinds of literature in the Bible than they do on others. Description of the different kinds of literature and the special interpretive principles for each are described in the next chapter.

5. Observe the Atmosphere

Observe the general tone of a passage. Is the mood joyful, sorrowful, thankful, concerned, angry, despairing, and so on? The author's words and setting shed light on the atmosphere. Paul's emphasis in Philippians on being joyful takes on added impact when one realizes he was writing from a Roman prison.

These basic principles of observation will help get you started. The important thing is to start studying the Bible and making whatever observations you can, asking as many questions as you can. When you know what questions to ask, the answers are often very rewarding.

Speed Bump!

Question **A**nswer

Q1. What is the foundation for Bible study?

A1. The foundation for Bible study is *spiritual* rebirth, a desire to know the Bible, an obedient heart, and a plan to learn.

Q2. What are the three keys to Bible study?

A2. The three keys to Bible study are *observation*, interpretation, and application.

Q3. Why is observation of the Bible so important?

A3. Observation is important, because unless we have observed correctly, we do not have *reliable* information.

Q4. How can we observe the Bible?

A4. We observe the Bible by developing a strategy that forces us to look *closely* at the text.

Fill in the Blank

Question
Answer

Q1. What is the foundation for Bible study?

A1. The foundation for Bible study is _____ rebirth, a desire to know the Bible, an obedient heart, and a plan to learn.

Q2. What are the three keys to Bible study?

A2. The three keys to Bible study are _____ , interpretation, and application.

Q3. Why is observation of the Bible so important?

A3. Observation is important, because unless we have observed correctly, we do not have _____ information.

Q4. How can we observe the Bible?

A4. We observe the Bible by developing a strategy that forces us to look _____ at the text.

For Further Thought and Discussion

1. What is the most difficult obstacle for you to overcome in studying the Bible? How do you think you can overcome it more effectively?

2. What is the most frustrating part of Bible study for you? Have you ever developed a methodical strategy for observing the biblical text? How do you think this chapter might help you?

3. Have you ever failed at a previous commitment to study the Bible? Why do you think you failed? Have you fallen victim to the tendency to set goals too high? Do you think you could set more modest goals to begin with and succeed at them? If so, what goals would you set?

What If I Don't Believe?

There is not much to disbelieve here. Either you think Bible study is not important or you do. If you don't, you are out of step with Scripture and need to reassess your whole understanding of how Christians grow spiritually, and your commitment to that. If you do agree that Bible study is important, experiment until you find something that works for you.

For Further Study

Other books which you will find important if you want to make the commitment to study the Bible regularly on your own are listed below in general order of difficulty, and present varying approaches. Your best choice would be to look at all of them in a Christian bookstore and try to get a feel for one of them before you try it.

- *The Joy of Discovery in Bible Study*, revised edition, Oletta Wald
- *Understanding Scripture*, revised edition, Berkeley Mickelsen and Alvera Mickelsen
- *Living by the Book*, Howard Hendricks
- *How to Study Your Bible*, Kay Arthur
- *Methodical Bible Study*, Robert Traina

There are national Bible-study approaches that you may be able to get involved with if nothing is available through your church. They are listed alphabetically below, and you can contact them to see if their Bible studies are going on in your area, or how to become involved. You may want to learn a little about each group's approach before actually trying one.

1. Bible Study Fellowship Intl.
   19001 Blanco Road
   San Antonio, TX 78258
   210/492-4676

2. Community Bible Study
   1765 Business Center Drive
   Suite 200
   Reston, VA 22090
   800/826-4181

3. Precept Ministries
   P.O. Box 182218
   Chattanooga, TN 37422-7218
   615/892-6814

4. Stonecroft Ministries (Christian Women's Clubs)
   Friendship Bible Coffee Dept.
   P.O. Box 9609
   Kansas City, MO 64134-0609
   816/763-7800

*If you believe what you like in the Gospel and
reject what you do not like, it is not the
Gospel you believe, but yourself.*
■ **St. Augustine**

How Can We Interpret
the Bible Accurately?

I have never forgotten William Blake's lines from "The Everlasting Gospel": "Both read the Bible day and night / But thou read'st
black where I read white." Doesn't that say it all? For some reason, two
people can read the same passage; one interprets it to say "black" but
the other, "white." Why is that?

One reason may lie in nature—the nature of people, and the nature of interpretation. It seems to me that humanity can be classified in
one of two large categories. I'm not sure what labels you give the categories, but one kind of person tends to take Scripture figuratively; the
other, quite literally. One person is flexible, tolerant, and open-
minded. The other is staunch, protective, and cautious. The one tends
to see gray. The other tends to see black and white.

I couldn't prove this if my life depended on it, but I believe that
people are inclined this way from birth, and that it affects everything
in their life, from political philosophy through social issues and to
morality and beyond. I don't believe one is right and the other wrong.
Both can have their own great strengths and terrible weaknesses. The
staunch person may defend the faith very well, while the tolerant person lets a crucial doctrine erode. On the other hand, the staunch person may spend his time fighting other Christians over things that
don't really matter, when he should be using his time and energy to
advance the cause of Christ among non-Christians. The tolerant person may be winning more people to Christ in one year than the
staunch person does in his entire lifetime. The key, it seems to me, is
to recognize and understand your own nature, capitalize on your
strengths, and try to avoid your weaknesses.

How does this relate to the interpretation of the Bible? For example, one person will read the description of Jesus in Revelation

chapter 1 as being exactly what Jesus looks like. His hair is dazzlingly white, His eyes flame like fire, His face looks as though it were sculpted from a lightning bolt. Another will say that the physical description symbolizes spiritual qualities of Christ. The dazzling light

The principles for interpreting the Bible are largely the same as for interpreting the U.S. Constitution or Caesar's writings.

stands for truth, the fire represents purity and holiness, and so forth. After all, how could Jesus talk if He had a literal sword coming out of His mouth? That and a hundred other passages are instinctively interpreted in a number of ways, depending on whether or not the person seems predisposed to interpret things literally or figuratively.

On the other hand, differences of interpretation arise simply because some people do not understand how to draw information from print. The same principles used to interpret the Bible are used to interpret the U.S. Constitution or the writings of Caesar. If we disregard those principles, we will misconstrue the meaning. So even in light of our natural tendency to interpret things differently, we can minimize faulty interpretation by knowing the principles of interpretation, which are what we want to look at in this chapter. First, we will consider human nature and how the nature of the written word itself necessitates interpretation. Next, we will examine general principles for Scripture interpretation. Finally, we will survey the different literary forms and how to interpret them.

Why Is Interpretation Necessary?

Interpretation is necessary because it is not always clear to us what a biblical writer meant by what he wrote.

From time to time one hears the protest, "Why do you have to interpret the Bible? Just read it and do what it says!" At one level, it is easy to understand and sympathize with this sentiment. The meaning of many biblical passages does seem straightforward. Furthermore, for most of us, our major problem with the Bible is not the parts that we *don't* understand but with the parts that we *do*—that is, in obeying such commands as "Do not repay evil for evil" (Romans 12:17) or "Be joyful in hope, patient in affliction, faithful in prayer" (Romans 12:12 NIV).

Other passages are not so straightforward. For example, when we read an English version of the Bible, we are already involved in interpretation. The final clause of 1 Corinthians 7:1 has been translated in varied ways such as: (a) "It is good for a man not to touch a woman" (KJV); (b) "It is a good principle for a man to have no physical contact with women" (PHILLIPS); (c) "It is a good thing for a man to have nothing to do with women" (NEB); (d) "It is good for a man not to marry" (NIV); and (e) "It is a good thing for a man not to touch a woman" (NAB). Note the NIV footnote, "It is good for a man not to have sexual relations with a woman," which expresses the ancient idiom "to touch a woman." So interpretation by the translators has already begun, even before we pick up an English Bible.

Also, all of us then bring to the Bible our own knowledge, attitudes, and beliefs about God, religion, and "reality," which will influence the way in which we construe the meaning of a biblical text. For example, when we read the word "church" we often think of a particular type of building, despite the facts that a biblical meaning of "church" is "the community of people who have placed their faith in Christ" and the early church met in homes rather than in church buildings for the first three hundred years of its existence.

> **The antidote to bad interpretation is not no interpretation, but good interpretation.**

In this chapter we learn that . . .

1. Interpretation is necessary because it is not always clear to us what a biblical writer meant by what he wrote.
2. Certain principles of interpretation must be followed for any passage of Scripture.
3. Each kind of literature has its own rules to be followed for correct interpretation.

Not only is interpretation unavoidable, but different interpreters do not always agree. "Bible-believing Christians" disagree about such things as the mode of baptism, whether one can lose his or her salvation, and the nature of restrictions on the participation of women in the church. Some Christians assert that God's will for all Christians is material prosperity on the basis of texts such as 3 John 2, "Beloved, I wish above all things that thou mayest prosper and be in health" (KJV) [usually omitting the qualification *"even as thy soul prospereth"* (emphasis added)], a verse that has nothing to do with financial prosperity. Many cults misread and distort the meaning of various biblical passages. However, as Gordon D. Fee and Douglas Stuart point out, "The antidote to bad interpretation is not no interpretation, but good interpretation based upon common-sense guidelines" (*How to Read the Bible for All Its Worth*, second edition 17).

The Bible is not a series of propositions and imperatives.

Interpretation is necessary not only because of who we are as readers but also because of the nature of Scripture itself. The Bible is the message of a changeless God and, as such, is timeless and always relevant. However, as Fee and Stuart explain, the Bible

is *not* a series of propositions and imperatives; it is not simply a collection of "Sayings from Chairman God," as though he looked down at us from heaven and said: "Hey you down there, learn these truths. Number 1, There is no God but One, and I am he. Number 2, I am the Creator of all things, including humankind"— and so on, all the way through proposition 7,777 and imperative 777 (emphasis theirs 18).

Although the Bible does contain these truths, they are not recorded in this form. "Throughout the Bible God becomes personally involved in people's lives. He doesn't offer pious platitudes but rather speaks directly to their needs in ways that are appropriate to their situations," Jack Kuhatschek says in *Taking the Guesswork Out of Applying the Bible* (29). God, through human authors, wrote the biblical texts to be timely to their original recipients. Therefore, the biblical texts address specific situations and questions. This historical particularity makes interpretation of the Bible challenging and fascinating.

Why I Need to Know This

If I don't understand that certain principles must be followed in the interpretation of Scripture, I am liable to draw wrong conclusions from what I read in the Bible. We cannot always know if we truly understand a difficult portion of Scripture, even with a proper understanding of the principles of interpretation. But without them, we can easily misunderstand even the simplest and most forthright passage.

The goal of Bible interpretation must be to understand what the author was trying to say to his original readers. As Gordon D.

Fee and Douglas Stuart note, "God's Word to us was first of all his Word to them" (18). They elaborate: *"A text cannot mean what it never meant.* Or to put it in a positive way, the true meaning of the biblical text for us is what God originally intended it to mean when it was first spoken. This is the starting point" (26). To understand what the Bible means, we must first understand what it meant to the original readers. This is hard, however, because of the distance of time, culture, and language between us and the first readers.

Time

The sixty-six books of the Bible were composed over a 1,500-year period that ended nineteen centuries ago. The world has changed a great deal since the last words were written, and without study we don't know what the world was like then. Without that knowledge, it is hard for us to understand what is at stake in many parts of the Bible. For example, it is hard to understand Jonah's unwillingness to obey God and preach in Nineveh until we learn that Nineveh was the most hated nation (and not just by Israel) of the eighth century B.C. It was a cross between Nazi Germany and the Mafia. Why should he want to help them?

A text cannot mean what it never meant.

Culture

Significant cultural distance separates us from the world of the biblical texts. For example, we cannot understand the book of Ruth apart from understanding the right and responsibility an available relative had to redeem the land of his dead relative and raise up a child to the childless widow. Also, writers living before the discovery of germs or molecules did not express truth in the ways and manners of modern scientists. If they had, their writings would have made no sense to anyone until our age arrived.

Geography

We are also geographically distant from the authors and recipients of the biblical books.

A knowledge of geography is helpful in understanding a passage such as John 2:11–13, in which Jesus had just been to a wedding in the Galilean town of Cana:

This beginning of His signs Jesus did in Cana of Galilee, and manifested His glory, and His disciples believed in Him. After this He went down to Capernaum, He and His mother, and His brothers, and His disciples; and there they stayed a few days. And the Passover of the Jews was at hand, and Jesus went up to Jerusalem (NASB).

Why did John say they went down to Capernaum from Cana, when Capernaum is north of Cana? And why did he say they went up to Jerusalem when Jerusalem is south of Capernaum? The answer is that we, in the modern world, are oriented to looking at maps with north being up and south being down. If we are in Florida, we say we are going up to New York. If we are in Washington, we say we are going down to California. But the ancients of Bible times did not have maps the way we do. When they said they went down from Cana to Capernaum, they meant they went *down!* That is, they descended in altitude. Cana is in the hills. Capernaum is on the shore of the Sea of Galilee, lower in altitude than Cana.

The Bible teaches truth in the ways and manners of expressing truth in ancient times.

When they went up to Jerusalem from Capernaum, John meant they went *up!* Approximately a thousand feet! When you are walking, you are acutely aware of what up and down are (down is easier). Knowing the location of the towns, the approximate terrain, the major bodies of water, and so forth helps a person visualize these verses, and they come to life. Without a knowledge of geography, these verses tend to lie lifeless on the page.

Language

Linguistic distance separates us from the biblical texts. The Old Testament was primarily written in ancient Hebrew, although there are a few passages in the related tongue of Aramaic. The New Testament was composed in Greek. The authors in each use words and phrases with which we are not totally familiar. As was pointed out earlier, the translation of the Scriptures into English itself requires interpretation.

In order to communicate His message as clearly as possible, God used many different forms of literature, including formal instruction, narration, parables, poetry and proverbs, and prophecy. Each of these literary forms has special principles that must be followed for proper interpretation. Before we examine the various forms of literature and the specific principles for interpreting them, let us look at general principles of interpretation that will help us understand any portion of Scripture.

What Can Help Me Interpret the Scriptures?

Certain principles of interpretation must be followed for any passage of Scripture.

As we said in the previous chapter on observation, spiritual rebirth, the illumination of the Holy Spirit, and an obedient heart are necessary to properly interpret the Bible. In 1 Corinthians 2:14 we read, "The man without the Spirit does not accept the things that come from the Spirit of God, for they are foolishness to him, and he cannot understand them because they are spiritually discerned" (NIV). This is not to say that non-Christians can understand nothing of the Bible's message, but they cannot understand its spiritual significance and be willing to obey the truth unless the Holy Spirit enlightens and convicts them. Even for Christians, diligent study, obedience, and submission to the truth of God's Word are necessary for spiritual understanding and insight (see Hebrews 5:12–14). As Walt Henrichsen summarizes in *A Layman's Guide to Interpreting the Bible:*

Without the Holy Spirit's help, no one understands spiritual truth.

> Seeing things from God's point of view is a ministry of the Holy Spirit to those who have not only trusted Him for salvation but for enlightenment as well. Though being a Christian is no guarantee that you will accurately interpret every passage in the Bible, it is foundational for properly understanding spiritual truth (27).

The Holy Spirit enlightens us as we prayerfully seek His guidance while following sound procedures of interpretation.

Literary context

The meaning of any passage of Scripture will be consistent with what comes before and after the passage. "Context" is important for several reasons.

A. Berkeley Mickelsen in *Interpreting the Bible* summarizes the importance of context as follows:

> Context is important because thought is usually expressed in a series of related ideas. Occasionally a person does make a swift and radical departure from the train of thought he is pursuing. Sometimes thoughts are tied together loosely by a general theme. But whether ideas are thus bound by close logical union or whether

the main propositions are developed by repetition, the meaning of any particular element is nearly always controlled by what precedes and what follows (100).

Too often we are guilty of "proof-texting," taking brief passages (often verses or portions of verses) out of context and quoting them in support of a doctrine or action. I will never forget, as a new Christian, how I used to take 1 Corinthians 2:9, "Eye has not seen, nor ear heard, / Nor have entered into the heart of man / The things which God has prepared for those who love Him," and wax eloquent on the glories of heaven. My ears flamed with embarrassment when the next verse was pointed out to me: "But God has revealed them to us through His Spirit." So! The "wonderful things that God has prepared for those who love Him" are not referring to heaven at all, but the spiritual blessings we have now through the revelation of the Holy Spirit. I had been innocently guilty of taking the passage out of context and making it say something the author never intended it to say.

Here is another example. A Christian counselor reported that a woman he was counseling told him that God revealed to her that she was to divorce her husband and marry another man (with whom she was romantically involved) on the basis of Paul's exhortation in Ephesians 4:24, "Put on the new man" (KJV) (H. L. Bussell, *Unholy Devotions* 119; cited in Klein *et al.* 7)! Give me a break! If we allow ourselves the freedom to take passages out of context, we can make the Bible say nearly anything we want it to say, even if it violently contradicts what the author originally meant.

Honoring the contexts of a passage keeps us from twisting Scripture.

Cults commonly cite verses out of context in order to claim biblical support for their erroneous beliefs and practices. Therefore, always make sure that the meaning of the passage you quote in support of a particular viewpoint has that meaning contextually. The smaller the passage you are studying, the greater is the likelihood of its being taken out of context. That is why the (modern) paragraph, which generally reflects a complete thought, is the basic unit of study.

Correct contextual interpretation of a passage involves examining:

- the immediate context;
- the book context;

- the context of other writings by the same author (if available);
- the context of the Testament you are studying (Old or New); and
- the entire Bible context.

The Bible will never contradict itself, either in the next paragraph, or in the previous paragraph.

The immediate context of a paragraph is usually the preceding two or three paragraphs and the subsequent two or three paragraphs. Chapter divisions are not inspired, and therefore are not always reliable boundary guides to immediate context, so don't be stopped by them when studying the context of a passage.

The smaller the passage, the more carefully you must examine its context.

Three types of information from the context can help interpret correctly a given passage. Does the interpretation fit the stated or apparent purpose of the book? Does it fit the flow of thought in the book? Do parallel passages shed any light on the passage you are studying? A parallel passage is any passage elsewhere in the Bible which deals with the same subject you are studying.

Historical-cultural Background

All the books of the Bible were written in a specific time and a specific place by a specific person for specific people. If we are going to understand what was written, it is often helpful to know as much as we can about the historical and cultural background of the writing. For example, in the letter to the church at Laodicea (Revelation 3:14–22), Christ condemns it for being "neither cold nor hot" and goes on to state "I wish you were either one or the other." Klein *et al.* explain that:

We must interpret "hot" and "cold" in light of the historical context of Laodicea, which was located close to both hot springs (by Hierapolis) and a cold stream (by Colossae). Now both hot and cold water are desirable; both are useful for distinct purposes. But the spiritual state of this church more closely resembled the tepid lukewarm water that eventually flowed into Laodicean pipes. Neither hot nor cold, it was putrid and emetic (causing vomiting). Jesus is *not* saying that active opposition to him (an incorrect interpretation of "cold") is better than being a lukewarm Christian (175–176).

It is not enough to be aware of historical facts and the customs of the particular cultural setting(s); the interpreter must be aware of the impact that the message would have had on the original audience. A modern audience is not surprised at the notion of a "Good Samaritan," but in Jesus' day there was such great hatred toward the Samaritans by Jews that the effect of His description would have been as unsettling as a present-day reference to a Good Terrorist.

> **Understood in its context, the notion of a Good Samaritan was as unsettling as the notion of a Good Terrorist is today.**

The interpretation of a passage must fit the historical-cultural situation of the book. It is more important to reconstruct the historical context than figure out the precise historical date. Use of tools such as a good Bible handbook can help you as you seek to fulfill the following interpretive goals (adapted from A. Berkeley Mickelsen, *Interpreting the Bible*):

- Know the people or peoples who are involved in the passage being interpreted.
- Determine what time period is the most likely.
- Check the place or places on a map.
- Note the customs, objects of material culture, or social-religious relationships that are in the story.
- Recognize how the history that took place before the times of the original hearers or readers influenced their responses and attitudes.
- Note not just similarities but also differences between the biblical story and the surrounding history and culture.
- Note similarities or differences in the degrees of precision and accuracy customary in matters of measurement and expression between the world of the biblical writer and readers in today's technical-scientific culture.
- Be aware of both similarities and differences between the historical-cultural situation of the original writer and readers, and your own historical-cultural situation (176).

Word Meanings

Each word has a range of meanings. For example, the English word "trunk" may refer to the main stem of a tree, a large piece of luggage, an elephant's nose, a person's torso, or the luggage compartment of an automobile. Also, words change meaning over time. The word that the King James Version several times translated in 1611 as "conversation" does not refer to "people talking" as we mean today; instead, today it means "manner of life" or "conduct." We must be sure the words we read in our Bible mean the same thing today. One of the easiest ways of doing this is to compare how different translations of the Bible treat a given word.

Which words merit more detailed study? Words that you don't understand, words that seem central to what the author is saying, and any words that are repeated or given special emphasis.

How do you study a word? First, determine the word's range of meaning. Bible encyclopedias discuss many important terms. Bible dictionaries shed much light on the meaning and usage of biblical words. Two good ones that do not require a knowledge of Greek and Hebrew are Vine's *Complete Expository Dictionary of Old and New Testament Words* and the *Nelson's New Illustrated Bible Dictionary*, edited by Ronald F. Youngblood. These tools give you the views of the scholars who wrote them. An exhaustive concordance of the Bible translation you use will enable you to examine all uses of a given word. A concordance lists every word in the Bible in alphabetical order, and the order in which it appears in the Bible. It is probably the most common Bible study tool a person will use in studying the Bible. Two concordances every Bible student should consider acquiring are the very portable *Nelson's Quick Reference® Bible Concordance* and the *New Strong's Exhaustive Concordance: Comfort Print Edition* (both published by Thomas Nelson).

After considering the possible meanings of the word, choose the meaning that best fits the immediate context. Check your study by reading a good commentary or two on the subject after you have finished your preliminary study. Suggestions for commentaries are given at the end of this book.

Grammar

We must pay attention to grammar as well, because words are put together to convey meaning according to rules of grammar. For example, in Ephesians 5:18 Paul exhorted the believers not to get drunk on wine (and be under its influence) but instead to "be filled with the Spirit." The use of the passive voice (rather than the active "fill yourself with the Spirit") indicates that the believer, rather than controlling himself, yields himself to the authority of the Spirit.

The biblical languages (Hebrew for the Old Testament, Greek for the New Testament) sometimes convey subtle meanings not found in English translations. For this reason it is helpful to consult one or two good commentaries *after doing one's own study of the passage.*

What Are the Guidelines for Interpreting Specific Kinds of Literature?

Each kind of literature has its own rules to be followed for correct interpretation.

Formal Instruction

Relatively straightforward presentation of the truth characterizes formal instruction, or *didactic* (meaning "to teach") literature. The highly organized explanation moves logically from point to point. Brief books using this literary form are often good starting points for learning personal Bible study skills because their meaning is usually easy to understand.

Paul's explanation of the gospel in Romans is a good example of formal instruction (didactic literature). Paul ties his argument together with the frequent use of transitional and connective words (such as *and, but, for,* and *therefore*) and of rhetorical questions (for example, 2:17–21, 26; 3:1, 3, 5; 4:1, 3, 9). Other biblical examples of the didactic form include the remaining epistles of Paul, as well as Hebrews; 1 and 2 Peter; 1, 2, and 3 John; and Jude.

Study the logical development of the argument.

The most important principle in interpreting this type of literature is to study the logical development of the argument. Try to understand the outline inherent in the chapter. As a second guideline, study the situation behind the statements. Each epistle arose out of and was intended for a specific first-century A.D. occasion. Understanding this occasion will help you to accurately perceive what particular passages meant to their original recipients as well as to validly apply their teachings today. If it is not apparent to you in your study, a good commentary will help.

Narration

Narrative literature emphasizes storytelling to relate a theological message. The Bible's continuing popularity results in part from the many fascinating stories in it. The first book of the Bible, Genesis (a name which means "Beginnings"), relates such stories as how God began the world, the flood and Noah's ark, the tower of Babel, how God began His plan to bless all peoples through the family of Abraham, and how He worked in the lives of the Hebrew patriarchs, Abraham, Isaac, Jacob, and Joseph. The second book, Exodus, picks up the story of this family, which has now become the nation of Israel, by telling how Moses leads them out of slavery in Egypt. The Old Testament books from Genesis through Ezra, the four Gospels, and Acts are classified as narrative literature. Stories, such as the one recorded in Isaiah 6, occur in many other books as well.

Pay close attention to the story's progress, to what changes and why.

As you read narrative literature, pay close attention to the plot. How does the story progress? Is the movement of the book primarily physical, spiritual, relational, geographical, or political? What has changed by the end of the book? Why?

Pay attention to the contributions of the characters and setting (time, geography, and social customs) to the plot. What theological truth(s) is the author attempting to convey through his selection of material? How might those truths be reflected in people's lives in our time and culture?

The Parable

Not everything in the Gospels belongs to the extended narrative form. The Gospels record many instances of Christ's use of the *parable* in order to teach. A typical definition of a parable is "a saying or story that seeks to drive home a point the speaker wishes to emphasize by illustrating it from a familiar situation of common life" (F. F. Bruce, *Zondervan Pictorial Encyclopedia of the Bible* 4:590). The word *parable* is used to refer to several different figures of speech, although the form Jesus used most frequently in His teaching is the story-parable. All parables, regardless of form, seek to communicate a spiritual truth by illustrating it with a situation with which the hearer was familiar.

Jesus' explanation of His use of parables (Matthew 13:11–15; Mark 4:10–12) indicates that He had two essential purposes. First, He was attempting to reveal truth to believers. Parables excel in vivid, memorable communication of the truth. Second, He was trying to conceal the truth from those whose hearts were already hardened against it.

Poetry and Proverbs

Poetry is found mainly in the books of Job, Psalms, Proverbs, Ecclesiastes, and Song of Solomon. However, poetry is scattered throughout other books. Hebrew poetry falls into three categories:

1. *Lyric poetry*—to be accompanied by music, like a song
2. *Instructional poetry*—to teach principles of living through pithy maxims
3. *Dramatic poetry*—to tell a story in poetic form

Understanding thought parallelism is the key to understanding all biblical poetry.

Hebrew poets used two main literary devices: parallelism, the matching of ideas; and figures of speech, or word pictures.

Parallelism. Rather than matching sounds, a Hebrew poet was more concerned with matching ideas. Six of the more common forms of parallelism are

1. *Synonymous parallelism*, which presents similar ideas:
   "Show me Your ways, O Lord;
   Teach me Your paths" (Psalm 25:4);
2. *Synthetic parallelism*, in which the second idea completes the first one:
   "The Lord is my shepherd;
   I shall not want" (Psalm 23:1);
3. *Antithetic parallelism*, in which the second thought contrasts with the first:
   "For the Lord knows the way of the righteous,
   But the way of the ungodly shall perish" (Psalm 1:6);
4. *Emblematic parallelism*, where the first line uses a figure of speech to illustrate the idea stated in the second line:
   "As the deer pants for the water brooks,
   So pants my soul for You, O God" (Psalm 42:1);
5. *Climactic parallelism*, where the second line repeats the first with the exception of the last word or words:
   "It is not for kings, O Lemuel,
   It is not for kings to drink wine" (Proverbs 31:4);

6. *Formal parallelism,* in which the lines of poetry must all exist for a complete thought:
"Yet I have set My King
On My holy hill of Zion" (Psalm 2:6).

Figures of Speech. Since the Hebrew poets wanted mental pictures to pop into the reader's mind, creating visual images was of prime consideration. They accomplished this with vivid figures of speech. Five of the most common figures of speech are

1. *Simile,* which compares two unlike things:
"Keep me as the apple of Your eye" (Psalm 17:8);
2. *Metaphor,* a comparison in which one thing is said to be another:
"The Lord is my shepherd" (Psalm 23:1);
3. *Hyperbole,* which deliberately overstates for the sake of emphasis:
"All night I make my bed swim;
I drench my couch with my tears" (Psalm 6:6);
4. *Rhetorical question,* which asks a question for the purpose of making a statement:
"Who can utter the mighty acts of the LORD,
Who can declare all His praise?" (Psalm 106:2);
5. *Personification,* which assigns the characteristics of a human to lifeless objects:
"The sun knows its going down" (Psalm 104:19).

These are the most notable among the figures of speech. In particular, the ones listed here express the visual imagery by which the Hebrew poets caused pictures to pop into the readers' minds.

If the reader keeps parallelism and figures of speech in mind when interpreting poetic literature, he understands this poetry much more readily.

Prophecy

Much of the Bible is prophetic. However, prophecy is not just the *foretelling* of the future; it is also the *forthtelling* of God's message to His people. In the Old Testament, the books from Isaiah to Malachi are prophetic; in the New Testament the book of Revelation is. Interpreting prophetic literature can be extremely difficult because so much symbolic, figurative, and non-literal material fills it, and we are not always told what the literal reality is behind the figurative language. A few guidelines, however, help greatly.

First, as with any passage in the Bible, study its history, context, and literal meaning. Study the historical

Prophecy both *forth-tells* and *fore*tells.

circumstances of both the prophet and the people to whom he prophesied. Carefully consider both the immediate and broad contexts. Take the words in their normal sense unless a figure of speech or a symbol is evidently being used, or unless the passage just doesn't make sense when taken literally. For example, Revelation talks of stars falling to the earth, and stars could not fall to the earth without obliterating it. So the stars must mean something other than literal stars.

Next, identify to whom the passage is written or what the passage is talking about. Is the passage forthtelling or foretelling? Has the prophecy been fulfilled? If it has been, study the writings that tell about the fulfillment. Is it still unfulfilled? If so, study it carefully and humbly. Unfulfilled prophecy is often very mysterious because of its use of symbolism. Since prophecy is so difficult, prophecy teachers can be helpful, but they can also be confusing since not all teachers agree on what symbolic language means. Different "schools" of opinion bring various perspectives to Bible prophecy, and it can be challenging but rewarding to become educated in this area.

Finally, remember that the main purpose of prophecy is not to inspire debate, tickle our curiosity, or fuel our opinions. Rather, its purpose is to encourage faith in God and to encourage holy living. For example, Paul introduces his discussion of the future

Holy living, not tickled curiosity, is the life aim of prophecy.

(1 Thessalonians. 4:13–18) by saying that he did not want the Thessalonian believers to be ignorant or to grieve as those who have no hope. In contrast to false teachers who evidently were teaching that their loved ones who died before Christ's return would not be raised to new life, Paul proclaimed that "the dead in Christ will rise first" (v. 16), and all believers "shall always be with the Lord. Therefore comfort one another with these words" (vv. 17–18).

God desires the promise of Christ's return to have a motivating and purifying effect on the personal life and ministry of Christians (see Titus 2:11–14), and not for its timing to become a source of conflict and division. Therefore, when you study biblical prophecy, always ask yourself, "How does God intend this truth to change my life?"

Conclusion

As we have said, the meaning of a given passage in the Bible is not always clear to us. There are three reasons. First, we bring to the interpretation certain assumptions that might not be correct. Second, a great gap of time, culture, and language results in some things written in the Bible being perfectly clear to the ones to whom it was written, and perfectly incomprehensible to us two or three thousand years later. Finally, all communication needs to be interpreted. I have even read things that I have written, and I no longer know what I meant by them. How much more might I be confused by someone else's writing! Oral language is usually accompanied by facial expressions, vocal inflections, and so forth. But you do not have these clues to interpretation with the written word. Therefore, when trying to master the word of God so that the word of God can master us, we must work hard at discovering what the Bible says and what it means.

Speed Bump!

Question Answer

Q1. Why is interpretation necessary?

A1. Interpretation is necessary because it is not always clear to us what a biblical writer *meant* by what he wrote.

Q2. What can help me interpret the Scriptures?

A2. Certain principles of interpretation must be followed for *any* passage of Scripture.

Q3. What are the guidelines for interpreting specific kinds of literature?

A3. Each kind of literature has its *own* rules to be followed for correct interpretation.

Fill in the Blank

Question Answer

Q1. Why is interpretation necessary?

A1. Interpretation is necessary because it is not always clear to us what a biblical writer _____ by what he wrote.

Q2. What can help me interpret the Scriptures?

A2. Certain principles of interpretation must be followed for
_____ passage of Scripture.

Q3. What are the guidelines for interpreting specific kinds of literature?

A3. Each kind of literature has its _____ rules to be followed for
correct interpretation.

For Further Thought and Discussion

1. Have you ever misunderstood a passage of Scripture, and later found
   out what the right understanding of it was? What was the cause of your
   original misunderstanding?

2. How great a role do you think "common sense" plays in interpreting
   Scripture? How much success do you think the average person has
   using a "common sense" approach to interpreting the Bible?

3. What parts of the Bible do you find easiest to understand? Why do you
   think that is the case?

What If I Don't Believe?

As in the case of "observation" of the Bible, there is not much to disbelieve in this chapter. Even people who take passages out of context usually
agree that it shouldn't be done. They just don't think they are doing it. To become an effective student of the Bible and avoid needless misinterpretation, it
is critical to take these principles seriously and interpret the Bible according to
sound rules.

For Further Study

Several other books helpful to the discipline of Bible study are listed below in general order of difficulty, beginning with the easiest.

Understanding Scripture, revised edition, Berkeley Mickelsen and Alvera
   Mickelsen
A Layman's Guide to Interpreting the Bible, Walter Henrichson
How to Read the Bible For All Its Worth, Gordon Fee and Douglas Stuart
Introduction to Biblical Interpretation, William Klein, Robert L. Hubbard,
   and Craig Blomberg

What makes the difference is not how many times you have been through the Bible, but how many times and how thoroughly the Bible has been through you.
■ Gypsy Smith

12

How Can We Apply the Bible Faithfully?

In his book *All Things Wise and Wonderful*, the Scottish veterinarian James Herriot, who must have been one of the twentieth century's best storytellers, chronicles his stint in the Royal Air Force during World War II. After months of rigorous conditioning, the airmen were nearing the end of their basic training. One day, hundreds of sunburned men dressed in dazzling white uniforms were lined up in a huge marching ground to hear an address by a visiting air commodore.

Before the dignitary arrived, a sergeant whom Herriot described as "lascivious" was leading the men in a succession of bawdy songs. Herriot later wrote:

I was intrigued by the reaction of the airman on my right. He was a slim, pink-faced lad of about nineteen and his lank fair hair fell over his face as he jumped up and down. He was really throwing himself into it, bawling out the indelicate words, duplicating the sergeant's [irreverent gestures] with maniacal glee. He was, I had recently learned, the son of a bishop.

They say that parsons' sons are a bit wild when let off the leash, and I suppose an escapee from a bishop's palace is even more susceptible to the blandishments of the big world. I looked at him again. All around him men were yelling their heads off, but his voice, mouthing the four-letter words with relish, rang above the rest and he followed the actions of the conducting sergeant like a devoted [disciple] (156–157).

Why is it that preacher's kids have such a reputation? Are they worse than other Christians' children, or are they simply more noticeable when they go "off the deep end?" Now I'm not coming down on preachers' kids. A little "preacher's kid" lurks in all of us, and I am not persuaded, from the preachers' kids I know, that they are any better or worse than other kids from Christian families. As a general rule, if kids are raised with a healthy dose of love balanced by discipline, with the parents involved in an affirming way in their lives, they tend to turn out well. But I have seen kids raised in that environment rebel wildly, and I have seen kids raised in bad environments turn out well.

In this chapter we learn that . . .

1. Application is important because God expects us not only to know the Bible, but to live it.

2. Application is difficult because spiritual growth takes time and because the world, our innate pull toward sin, and the devil all militate against it.

3. We can apply the Bible by studying it diligently, taking its teachings seriously, and committing ourselves to do all that we understand of what God wants of us.

4. We can increase our chances of changing by deciding to change and by following a specific plan to change.

No, my goal is not to analyze preachers' kids, but to use the example as a launching pad for a discussion of the application of Scripture. Why is it that some people have their heads full of the Bible, but it makes no difference in their hearts? Why is it that the longest road to travel is the distance from knowing something good to doing something good? The Bible is not intended to be a book to satisfy our curiosity but to change our lives. Its goal is not to make us knowledgeable; its goal is to make us holy. One of my seminary professors used to say "The Bible was not given to make us more intelligent sinners, but to change our lives." Whenever we see someone who is not living a holy life, whether it is a preacher's kid or anyone else raised with a knowledge of biblical truth, something is wrong. Something has gone amiss. And, if we are ministering to others, our task is to disciple others not only to know Christ's commands but also to obey them.

The Bible is not for satisfying curiosity, but for changing lives.

Why Is Application So Important?

Application is important because God expects us not only to know the Bible,
but to live it.

Joshua 1:8 says:

This Book of the Law shall not depart from your mouth, but you
shall meditate in it day and night, that you may observe to do according to all that is written in it. For then you will make your way
prosperous, and then you will have good success.

Several important observations can be made about this passage. First, the book of the Law is not to depart from our mouths,
meaning we are to talk about it regularly. But if we talk about it
regularly, we must think about it regularly (you shall meditate on
it day and night). We will never talk about the word unless we are
thinking about the word. Those important observations should
encourage us to read, study, memorize, meditate on, and talk
about the Bible. However, that is not enough for success in life.
Success, as this passage declares, is not a matter of talking about
the word, thinking about the word, and knowing the word. Success results from doing the word (that you may observe to do according to all that is written in it). Only as we obey the word do
we have the promise that our way will be prosperous, and that
we will have good success.

The night before His death Jesus told His apostles, "If you
know these things, blessed are you if you do them" (John 13:17).
James 1:22–25 both reinforces and expands upon these words:

Do not merely listen to the word, and so deceive yourselves. Do
what it says. Anyone who listens to the word but does not do
what it says is like a man who looks at his face in a mirror and, after looking at himself, goes away and immediately forgets what
he looks like. But the man who looks intently into the perfect law
that gives freedom, and continues to do this, not forgetting what
he has heard, but doing it—he will be blessed in what he does.
(NIV)

On the other hand, from God's perspective knowledge without obedience is sin. James 4:17 states, "Therefore, to him who
knows to do good and does it not, to him it is sin." Furthermore,
if you don't act on your spiritual understanding and insight, you

lose it (cf. Matthew 13:12–15). This was the problem of the believers who were addressed in Hebrews 5:11–14: though they had

Obedience leads to more insight and growth.

had plenty of time to become spiritually mature and should have become teachers by that point, they were instead spiritual infants because they had not been applying the truth which they had "learned." Fortunately, obedience to the truth leads to increased spiritual insight and growth: "For whoever has, to him more will be given, and he will have abundance" (Matthew 13:12).

Remember that in the New Testament, God desires that His word be written on our hearts, meaning that "our innermost being takes on the character of Scripture, which is the character of God himself. From God's heart to Scripture to our hearts is the divinely intended sequence" (Jack Kuhatschek, *Taking the Guesswork out of Applying the Bible* 25). Though total character transformation will not occur until we see Christ face to face (1 John 3:1–3), the process has already begun.

Why Is Application So Difficult?

Application is difficult because spiritual growth takes time and because the world, our innate pull toward sin, and the devil all militate against it.

Some parts of the Bible seem irrelevant to our lives today. Other sections we don't even understand. Still other portions are understandable and sound good when we hear a preacher expound on them, but when we try to live them, the reward of spiritual growth happens so slowly that we lose concentration or motivation. Yet the Bible does pertain to today, and obedience to it honors God. Jesus asserted, "Whoever has my commands and obeys them, he is the one who loves me. He who loves me will be loved by my Father, and I too will love him and show myself to him" (John 14:21 NIV). In 1 Corinthians 10:6 Paul referred to the wilderness wanderings of Israel (recorded in Exodus and Numbers) when he stated, "these things became our examples, to the intent that we should not lust after evil things as they also lusted." He extended the point to the whole Old Testament in Romans 15:4 when he declared, "For everything that was written in the past was written to teach us, so that through endurance and the encouragement of the Scriptures we might have hope" (NIV). Second Timothy 3:16–17 proclaims, "All Scripture is God-breathed and is useful for teaching, rebuking, correcting and training in righteousness, so that the man of God may be thoroughly equipped for every good work" (NIV). All Scripture is both inspired and relevant.

This fact does not mean that every single verse will have dramatic significance for us. When I was attending a Christian college, shortly after my conversion, great attention was given to Isaiah 3:21 as a prime verse for classes which required Scripture memory. It says, simply, "finger rings, nose rings." Admittedly, that verse could not be expected to impact dramatically a high percentage of readers. However, the verse numberings in our present Bible were not in the original writings. The point is, every sentence or every verse is part of a larger unit of thought which is inspired and has some relevance for us.

Scripture sometimes seems irrelevant because it is so specific to the people to whom it was written, and their situations, questions, and concerns are not always our situations, questions, and concerns. However, the Bible is not only timely, it is also timeless with an eternal relevance.

How Can We Apply the Bible?

We can apply the Bible by studying it diligently, taking its teachings seriously, and committing ourselves to do all that we understand of what God wants of us.

Howard and William Hendricks aptly comment, "Observation plus interpretation without application equals abortion. In other words, every time you observe and interpret but fail to apply, you perform an abortion on the Scriptures in terms of their purpose" (*Living by the Book*, 283–284). At this step in the process of Bible study you ask questions such as: How should my life change as a result of the truth(s) in a particular text? What must I do? What must I believe?

Ask yourself the questions Howard and William Hendricks suggest:

• Is there an example to follow?
• a sin to avoid?
• a promise to claim?
• a prayer to repeat?

- a command to obey?
- a condition to meet?
- an error to mark? or
- a challenge to face? (304)

The key to application involves discovering in a text "the spiritual, moral, or theological principles that have relevance for the contemporary believer" (Henry A. Virkler, *Hermeneutics* 212).

As Kuhatschek points out, Jesus Himself emphasized the importance of understanding the general principles that lie behind specific biblical teachings (52–54). The Jewish rabbis had counted 613 commandments in the Law of Moses. These teachers debated whether some commands were greater in the sense that obeying them necessarily entailed obedience of the "lesser commandments." When Jesus was asked which of the commandments was greatest, He responded:

> " 'Love the Lord your God with all your heart and with all your soul and all your mind.' This is the first and greatest commandment. And the second is like it: 'Love your neighbor as yourself.' *All the Law and the Prophets hang on these two commandments*" (Matthew 22:37–39 NIV, emphasis mine).

In other words, the commands to love God and others were general principles under which the other 611 laws could be placed. These other 611 commandments gave specific instructions on what to do to love God and what to do to love your neighbor as yourself.

Why I Need to Know This

I need to know this because application of the Bible is the third leg of a three-legged stool. The stool is useless without three legs. Observation and interpretation are worthless unless they result in application. Therefore, I need to regard application as critically important to the Christian life, and must also understand how to make effective applications from the Bible.

Some specifics of how to express love in our society will differ. For example, Leviticus 19:9–10 commands: "When you reap the harvest of your land, do not reap to the very edges of your-field or gather the gleanings of your harvest. Do not go over your vineyard a second time or pick up the grapes that have fallen. Leave them for the poor and the alien" (NIV). These commands limited the wasting of food and made it possible for the physically able though poor to obtain food through personal effort. Although this would be difficult to do today, we can find ways of obeying the spirit of this command.

How can we know whether the original commandments are universal principles that bind us today? While no formula guarantees a correct answer, the following questions are helpful.

1. Is the passage general or specific? Does it apply to everyone, or just to the person to whom it was written, as when Paul wrote to Timothy to "bring the cloak that I left with Carpus at Troas when you come—and the books, especially the parchments" (2 Timothy 4:13). That is a clearly specific command which we don't need to obey. But we might see a more practical principle behind this specific injunction, namely that practical measures that meet physical needs result in genuine and important ministry.

2. Does the passage pertain only to a cultural issue of the day, or does it also apply today? For example, commands not to eat things offered to idols would be relevant to very few people in the Western world today.

3. Has the passage been superseded by a newer or broader teaching? For example, the Old Testament command to keep Saturday holy does not apply to us today, because the New Testament example was to meet on the first day of the week, Sunday (1 Corinthians 16:2; Acts 20:7).

4. If the passage clearly states a universal truth and that truth is reiterated, then we are to obey it today. For example, the Ten Commandments tell us not to murder, and the New Testament repeats the command. This makes it pretty clear that we are not to murder!

5. Some passages clearly apply to us today, and some passages clearly won't. Many others can be legitimately debated. We need to understand that and not be discouraged if we waver over a given passage.

To apply *Old Testament commands,* consider first whether the command was either restated or revoked in the New Testament. We no longer need to follow revoked commands. For example, Christ's once-for-all sacrifice fulfilled the Old Testament sacrificial laws (Hebrews 9–10). However, nine of the Ten Commandments are restated in the New Testament, so they are binding today. What about commands that are not directly restated or revoked, such as the commandment to keep the Sabbath? In these cases, consider the principle behind the law. For example, in addition to attending church worship services you might set aside time(s) during the week for rest and special reflection upon God and His goodness to you.

To apply most *New Testament commands,* simply follow the **Nine of the Ten Commandments are restated in the New Testament.** general guidelines for application discussed above. After you understand the original circumstances, determine if yours is identical or comparable to it. If your condition is the same, you can apply the command directly. If the situation is not identical, determine the principle behind the command and apply it to situations you face.

What about biblical *examples?* How do we know what to emulate and what to avoid? When the Bible explicitly holds someone up as an example, note whether the author presents the person as a positive or negative example and what is said about him. When the Bible is not explicit about whether a person is a good or bad example and in what respects, then you must evaluate their stories based on truths or principles taught elsewhere in Scripture.

Finally, how do you determine how to validly apply biblical *promises?* First, is the promise part of the Old Covenant or the New Covenant? If the former, the promise may not directly apply to us. For example, in Malachi 3:10, we read, "Bring all the tithes into the storehouse, that there may be food in My house, and try Me now in this," says the Lord of hosts. "If I will not open for you the windows of heaven and pour out for you such blessing that there will not be room enough to receive it."

This is often used today as a promise that if we will but tithe our money, God will return abundant material wealth to us. However, this promise was given to the nation of Israel under the Mosaic law. That law was fulfilled in Jesus, and the commands of it are not transferred to the church. The church is certainly instructed to give financial support to the work of the Lord (2 Corinthians 8—9), but nowhere are we instructed in the New Testament to bring food into the house of God (there is no house of God in the New Testament other than believers, in whom God abides, 1 Peter 2:5), and nowhere are we promised material blessing for financial generosity.

Principles from Malachi 3:10 do apply to us today. For example, God rewards obedience (Matthew 5:12, 1 Corinthians 3:14), and we should give back a portion of our income to the Lord as an act of worship and obedience (1 Corinthians 16:1, 2 Corinthians 8—9).

If the promise is a New Testament one, then it may or may not apply to us, depending on the answers to other questions. First, to whom is the promise given? As Kuhatschek points out, at least three categories of promises are directly intended for us: those universal in scope (Romans 10:13; 1 John 2:2), those given to the church (Matthew 28:20; Romans 8:28), or those given to other groups to which we belong (Ephesians 6:1–3). When promises are made that were not directly intended for us, we must ask if other Scripture gives us reasons for believing that the promises apply to us in a secondary sense.

We must also ask if the promise is conditional or unconditional. Many promises in the Scripture have at least one condition attached to them. We cannot expect the promise to be given if we do not fulfill the condition. For example, we want God's peace to rule our lives, yet there are clear conditions for this. In Philippians 4:7 we are promised that the peace of God, which surpasses all understanding, will guard our hearts and minds through Christ Jesus. However, the condition for this peace is found in 4:6, "Be anxious for nothing, but in everything by prayer and supplication, with thanksgiving, let your requests be made known to God." We cannot have the promise without fulfilling the condition.

> **We cannot expect to receive promises if we refuse to meet their conditions.**

How Can We Increase Our Chances of Changing?

We can increase our chances of changing by deciding to change and by following a specific plan to change.

Once you have determined what a passage means to you, how do you accomplish the change that you desire? How do you get from good intentions to a transformed life? It is worth reiterating that the Holy Spirit is the agent of change in the life of a Christian. We must depend on Him, pray for change, and cultivate an obedient heart. But at the same time, we must involve ourselves in a process that will encourage the desired change.

Howard and William Hendricks suggest a three-step process (324–330). *First, decide to change,* and determine how you will be different after making the change. The key here is stating a clear, observable, and measurable objective referring to a realistic behavioral change. The Hendrickses comment:

> Clearly defined objectives help us see truth as actions, not abstractions. Likewise, they keep our expectations on the ground, within reach. Is your aim to develop the compassion of a Mother Teresa? Wonderful. But don't make that your objective. A better place to start is with a soup kitchen in your own community. Determine some practical ways to meet their needs. That's achievable. That's something you can do right now. That's a realistic step in the right direction (327).

Second, come up with a plan. This means devising "specific ways to achieve an objective and then thinking through what you need to do to run the plan. It assigns names, dates, times, and places to your intentions. The more specific your plan, the more likely it is that you'll succeed in it" (328).

Third, follow through. Get started! The ancient Chinese sage Lao-tzu said, "A journey of a thousand miles begins with a single step." Take the first step! Also, establish ways to help you carry through with the commitment to change you have made in obedience to God's Word.

The Hendrickses suggest three helpful strategies in this regard. First, use a checklist, particularly if your plan calls for either repeated steps or a series of progressive steps. One benefit from this procedure is the added motivation that it will provide as you establish "memorial stones" to mark your progress.

Second, set up relationships involving accountability. This could be through informal means such as talking about your goals, progress, and struggles with a spouse or close friend, or joining a formal accountability group.

Third, regularly evaluate your progress through keeping a journal, scheduling regular times of personal reflection, and so on.

Conclusion

Learning all the ins and outs of Bible study can be a complicated process and can take a long time to get familiar with. The important thing is not to let the process overwhelm you. When I first became a Christian, the gentleman who led me to the Lord gave me a New Testament, and told me to read the Gospel of John six times. Then, I was to begin at the beginning and read the whole New Testament clear through. He told me to underline the things I understood and that made sense to me. He encouraged me to write in the margins anything that I needed to change, and then to pray to God to help me change it.

Since that time I have had nearly twelve years of formal theological education. I have studied Bible study methods, I have taught Bible study methods, and I am writing a book which includes Bible study methods. My advice for the beginner follows.

First, begin. Start on a level that is meaningful to you, and climb from there as your understanding increases. Since I finished my formal theological education, I have had over twenty years of ministry experience. I still find my original method very fruitful. I read the Bible regularly, concentrating on the things I do understand and know apply to me today. Mark Twain once said something like, "Most people are bothered by the things in the Bible they don't understand. Frankly, the things that bother me are the ones I do understand." I'm the same way. I am still working on "Love the Lord your God with all your heart and with all your soul and with all your mind, . . . love your neighbor as yourself" (Matthew 22:37–39 NASB). I am still working on "Do not love the world or the things in the world. If anyone loves the world, the love of the Father is not in him. For all that is in the world—the lust of the flesh, the lust of the eyes, and the pride of life—is not of the Father but is of the world" (1 John 2:15–16). I am still working on "I beseech you therefore, brethren, by the mercies of God, that you present your bodies a living sacrifice, holy, acceptable to God, which is your reasonable service. And do not be conformed to this world, but be transformed by the renewing of your mind, that you may prove what is the good and acceptable and perfect will of God" (Romans 12:1–2). I am convinced that if

> **Concentrate on what you do understand and can apply.**

we were faithful to everything that we do understand from the Bible, we would have much less difficulty dealing with the passages we don't understand.

The second thing I advise is to get good teaching. The Bible is such an enormous and difficult book that very few of us can gain a good understanding of it without solid Bible **Study with a good** teaching. When looking for good teachers, look **Bible teacher.** for two things. First, make sure they are not teaching something entirely new. In the basic body of information that all orthodox Christians have agreed on and believed for the last two thousand years, there is not likely to be something really big and entirely new. These "fundamentals of the faith" need to be foundational in anyone from whom you learn. The fundamentals would include:

- A holy God exists who is the creator of all that is.
- Jesus, the Son of God, is also divine, and came to earth to die for our sins.
- The Holy Spirit is also God, and has an active ministry in our lives today.
- This one God exists eternally in three persons, God the Father, God the Son, and God the Holy Spirit. They are the same in substance but distinct in subsistence. There is no God other than this triune God.
- Humans are separated from God because of their sin, and must be saved from their lost condition since they cannot save themselves. Salvation is available by grace through faith in Jesus Christ. By repenting of our sin and committing our lives to following Jesus, we are given eternal life by God.
- The Bible is the word of God, verbally and totally inspired by God and without error in the original manuscripts. There is no Scripture but the Bible.
- Christians are to band together in local churches to worship God, to build one another up in the faith, to carry the message of salvation to the world, and to be humanitarian to those in need.
- Jesus is returning someday. We are to give people this hope, warn others of the dangers of dying without Christ, and live in hope and purity of life ourselves.

Your Bible teacher should hold to these fundamentals of the faith. He should also be a person of high moral and ethical integrity. A person lax in either morals or ethics is not worthy to be followed as a Bible teacher. Even within these very broad boundaries, there are good Bible teachers and poor ones. The Holy Spirit must guide you as you pray for a good Bible teacher. But remember, you can also be taught by books, audio tapes, video tapes, and television and radio. Wonderful Bible teachers in each of these areas can be of great benefit. Be discerning, because there are also poor and bad Bible teachers in each of these media. Rely heavily on prayer and the guidance of the Holy Spirit. Do not depend entirely on nonpersonal teaching, however, for God never intended us to make it alone. He wants us to become involved in the lives of others who believe as we do.

Observation, interpretation, and application: Those are the three keys to mastering the Bible and having the Bible master us.

Speed Bump!

Question **A**nswer

Q1. Why is application so important?

A1. Application is important because God expects us not only to know the Bible, but to *live* it.

Q2. Why is application so difficult?

A2. Application is difficult because spiritual growth takes time and because the world, our innate pull toward sin, and the devil all *militate* against it.

Q3. How can we apply the Bible?

A3. We can apply the Bible by studying it diligently, taking its teachings seriously, and *committing* ourselves to do all that we understand of what God wants of us.

Q4. How can we increase our chances of changing?

A4. We can increase our chances of changing by *deciding* to change and by following a specific plan to change.

Fill in the Blank

Question **A**nswer

Q1. Why is application so important?

A1. Application is important because God expects us not only to know the Bible, but to _____ it.

Q2. Why is application so difficult?

A2. Application is difficult because spiritual growth takes time and because the world, our innate pull toward sin, and the devil all _____ against it.

Q3. How can we apply the Bible?

A3. We can apply the Bible by studying it diligently, taking its teachings seriously, and _____ ourselves to do all that we understand of what God wants of us.

Q4. How can we increase our chances of changing?

A4. We can increase our chances of changing by _____ to change and by following a specific plan to change.

For Further Thought and Discussion

1. Why do you think people like the bishop's son in the opening story don't make the transition from knowing the Bible to living it?

2. What is the biggest obstacle in your life to applying the Bible?

3. What is the greatest help you know of in applying the Bible?

What If I Don't Believe?

If I don't believe the information in this chapter, I am liable not to commit myself to becoming a serious Bible student. If I am exposed to biblical truth, I may not commit my life to conforming to it. I may not rely on the Holy Spirit to lead me into truth and help me change. Learning and following the Bible can be very rewarding, and helping others do the same can also be very rewarding, but if I don't believe the material in this chapter, I am not likely to make the effort.

For Further Study

Books which will help you in your study of this subject include the following:

30 Days to Understanding What Christians Believe, Max Anders
30 Days to Understanding How to Live as a Christian, Max Anders
Taking the Guesswork Out of Applying the Bible, Jack Kuhatschek

Bibliography

Anders, Max E. *30 Days to Understanding the Bible*, Dallas: Word, Inc., 1992. *Thirty Days to Understanding How to Live as a Christian*, Dallas, Word, Inc., 1994. *Thirty Days to Understanding What Christian's Believe*, Dallas, Word, Inc., 1994.

Bloom, Allan. *The Closing of the American Mind*. New York: Simon & Schuster, 1987.

Colson, Charles. *Loving God*. Grand Rapids: Zondervan, 1987.

Fee, Gordon D., and Douglas Stuart. *How to Read the Bible for All Its Worth* (2nd ed.). Grand Rapids: Zondervan, 1993.

Frye, Northrop. *The Great Code: The Bible and Literature*. New York: Harcourt, 1983.

Graham, Billy. *How to Be Born Again*. Dallas: Word, Inc., 1989.

Green, Michael P. *Illustrations for Biblical Preaching*. Grand Rapids: Baker Book House Co., 1988.

Hendricks, Howard G., and William D. Hendricks. *Living by the Book*. Chicago: Moody Press, 1993.

Henrichsen, Walter A. *A Layman's Guide to Interpreting the Bible*. Grand Rapids: Zondervan, 1985.

Herriot, James. *All Things Wise and Wonderful*. New York: St. Martin's Press, 1977.

Kennedy, James. "The Bible: Fable, Fraud or Fact," Coral Ridge Video Ministry (January 4, 1994).

Klein, William W., and Craig L. Bomberg. *Introduction to Biblical Interpretation*. Dallas: Word, Inc., 1993.

Kuhatschek, Jack. *Taking the Guesswork Out of Applying the Bible*. Downer's Grove, IL: InterVarsity Press, 1990.

Lindsell, Harold. *God's Incomparable Word*. Minneapolis: World Wide Publications, 1978.

McDowell, Josh. *Evidence that Demands a Verdict*. Nashville: Thomas Nelson Publishers, 1992.

Mickelsen, A. Berkeley. *Interpreting the Bible*. Grand Rapids: Eerdmans, 1963.

Mickelsen, A. Berkeley, and Alvera M. Mickelsen. *Understanding Scripture* (rev. ed.). Peabody, MA: Hendrickson Pubs., Inc., 1992.

Packer, James I. *God Has Spoken*. Grand Rapids: Baker Book House Co., 1994.

Ryken, Leland. "The Literary Influence of the Bible," in *A Complete Literary Guide to the Bible* (eds., Leland Ryken and Tremper Longman III). Grand Rapids: Zondervan, 1993.

Sivan, Gabriel (ed.). *The Bible and Civilization*. New York: Times Books, 1974.

Traina, Robert A. *Methodical Bible Study*. Grand Rapids: Zondervan, 1985.

Virkler, Henry A. *Hermeneutics*. Grand Rapids: Baker Book House Co., 1981.

Wald, Oletta. *The Joy of Teaching Discovery Bible Study* (rev. ed.). Minneapolis: Augsburg, 1975.

Master Review

Chapter 1

Q1. What influence has the Bible had on our society?

Question
Answer

A1. The Bible has played a major role in determining the social *values* of the Western world.

Q2. What influence has the Bible had on our culture?

A2. The Bible has been a dominant influence in the *arts* of the Western world.

Q3. What influence has the Bible had on our spiritual life?

A3. The Bible has been a dominant influence in the spiritual, moral, and ethical *formation* of the Western world.

Chapter 2

Q1. Does the Bible contain errors?

A1. The Bible as originally written was *without error*.

Q2. Are the Bible manuscripts reliable?

A2. The Bible that we have today says essentially the *same* thing that the original Bible said.

Q3. How does archaeology testify to the accuracy of the Bible?

A3. Not one archaeological find disproves accounts in the Bible and many *confirm* the historical accuracy of the Bible.

Q4. Does fulfilled prophecy testify to the identity of the Bible as the word of God?

A4. The fulfilled prophecies of the Bible lend powerful *support* to its being the word of God.

Q5. Do changed lives testify to the truth of the Bible?

A5. The hearts of multiplied millions of people throughout the last two thousand years have been *transformed* by the Bible, lending weight to its being the word of God.

Chapter 3

Q1. How did God communicate His truth to us?

A1. Through several means, God *revealed* to us the information He wanted us to know.

Q2. How did fallible men record an infallible message?

A2. God supernaturally *inspired* the writing of the Scriptures so that the writer, in his own personality, composed and recorded without error God's revelation in the original manuscripts or letters.

Q3. How can humans understand divine information?

A3. The Holy Spirit *illumines* the mind of the obedient believer to understand increasingly the spiritual truth of the Scripture.

Q4. How was the Bible finally compiled?

A4. God sovereignly *oversaw* the process of the church's recognizing the books and letters which God had inspired and collecting them into one book, the Bible.

Chapter 4

Q1. How has the Bible been viewed by those who reject Christianity?

A1. Some view the Bible solely as a product of *human* insight, and reject it as being the word of God.

Q2. How has the Bible been viewed by those who think that part but not all of the Bible is the word of God?

A2. Some people believe that, while not all the Bible is the word of God, the Bible *contains* the word of God.

Q3. How has the Bible been viewed by those who accept Christianity and the Bible as the word of God?

A3. Although areas of the Bible have been historically contested, all Christians have historically *agreed* on a large body of truth.

Chapter 5

Q1. What is the capsule summary of the Old Testament?

A1. The Old Testament is primarily the story of God's dealings with humanity through the nation of *Israel*.

Q2. What are the major eras of Old Testament history?

A2. The entire story of the Old Testament can be broken into *nine* major time periods.

Q3. What was the geographical movement of the Old Testament?

A3. The geographical focus of the Israelites *moved* from Ur (where Abraham first lived), to Canaan (patriarchs), to Egypt (slavery), back to Canaan (which became Israel under the monarchy), to Babylonia (captivity) and back to Jerusalem (return).

Chapter 6

Q1. What is the capsule summary of the New Testament?

A1. The New Testament is primarily the story of Jesus' dealings with humanity through the *church*.

Q2. What are the major eras of New Testament history?

A2. The entire story of the New Testament can be broken into *three* major time periods.

Q3. What was the geographical movement of the New Testament?

A3. The geographical focus of the New Testament *moved* from Bethlehem to Jerusalem to Capernaum and back to Jerusalem; then to Asia Minor and Greece.

Chapter 7

Q1. What is the message of the Bible?
A1. The message of the Bible is that God is *demonstrating* to the universe through us that He is who He says He is.
Q2. What is the focus of the Old Testament?
A2. The Old Testament focuses on the *temporary* solution God provided to humanity's sin problem.
Q3. What is the focus of the New Testament?
A3. The New Testament focuses on the *permanent* solution God has provided in Christ to humanity's sin problem.

Chapter 8

Q1. What is God's strategy for relating to humanity?
A1. *Four* main elements comprise God's strategy for relating to humanity: revelation, faith, blessing, and reproduction.
Q2. How was God's strategy for relating to humanity executed in the Old Testament?
A2. God worked through the nation of Israel, promising *earthly* reward for trusting obedience.
Q3. How was God's strategy for relating to humanity executed in the New Testament?
A3. God worked through the church, promising *spiritual* reward for trusting obedience.
Q4. What are the consequences of faithful obedience to God?
A4. Our faithful obedience to God results in God's *glory*, our blessing, and a witness to the world.

Chapter 9

Q1. How is the Bible like a mirror?
A1. The Bible is like a mirror in that it accurately *reflects* our spiritual appearance.
Q2. How is the Bible like a sword?
A2. The Bible is like a sword in that it can be used as a *weapon* both to defend us and attack the enemy.
Q3. How is the Bible like light?
A3. The Bible is like light in that it enables us to *see* in the darkness of life so that we stay on the right path and avoid harm.
Q4. How is the Bible like water?

A4. The Bible is like water in that it quenches our *thirst* and cleanses us from spiritual impurities.

Q5. How is the Bible like food?

A5. The Bible is like food in that it satisfies our spiritual *hunger*, and causes us to grow.

Chapter 10

Q1. What is the foundation for Bible study?

A1. The foundation for Bible study is *spiritual* rebirth, a desire to know the Bible, an obedient heart, and a plan to learn.

Q2. What are the three keys to Bible study?

A2. The three keys to Bible study are *observation*, interpretation, and application.

Q3. Why is observation of the Bible so important?

A3. Observation is important, because unless we have observed correctly, we do not have *reliable* information.

Q4. How can we observe the Bible?

A4. We observe the Bible by developing a strategy that forces us to look *closely* at the text.

Chapter 11

Q1. Why is interpretation necessary?

A1. Interpretation is necessary because it is not always clear to us what a biblical writer *meant* by what he wrote.

Q2. What can help me interpret the Scriptures?

A2. Certain principles of interpretation must be followed for *any* passage of Scripture.

Q3. What are the guidelines for interpreting specific kinds of literature?

A3. Each kind of literature has its *own* rules to be followed for correct interpretation.

Chapter 12

Q1. Why is application so important?

A1. Application is important because God expects us not only to know the Bible, but to *live* it.

Q2. Why is application so difficult?

A2. Application is difficult because spiritual growth takes time and because the world, our innate pull toward sin, and the devil all *militate* against it.

Q3. How can we apply the Bible?

A3. We can apply the Bible by studying it diligently, taking its teachings seriously, and *committing* ourselves to do all that we understand of what God wants of us.

Q4. How can we increase our chances of changing?

A4. We can increase our chances of changing by *deciding* to change and by following a specific plan to change.

About the Author

Max Anders is a pastor at heart who applies the truths of God's word to people's everyday lives. An original team member with Walk Thru the Bible Ministries and pastor of a mega-church for a number of years before beginning his speaking and writing ministry, Max has traveled extensively, speaking to thousands across the country.

His books include *30 Days to Understanding the Bible, 30 Days to Understanding the Christian Life, 30 Days to Understanding What Christians Believe.* He holds a Master of Theology degree from Dallas Theological Seminary and a doctorate from Western Seminary in Portland, Oregon.

If you are interested in having Max Anders speak at your conference, church, or special event, please call interAct Speaker's Bureau at 1-800-370-9932.